D1261120

FASHIONOPOLIS

The SECRETS Behind
the Clothes We Wear

FASHIONOPOLIS

The SECRETS Behind the Clothes We Wear

YOUNG READERS EDITION

DANA THOMAS

DIAL BOOKS FOR YOUNG READERS

Dial Books for Young Readers
An imprint of Penguin Random House LLC, New York

First published in the United States of America by Dial Books for Young Readers,
an imprint of Penguin Random House LLC, 2022

Copyright © 2022 by Dana Thomas

Visit us online at penguinrandomhouse.com.

Library of Congress Cataloging-in-Publication Data is available.

Book manufactured in Canada

ISBN 9780593325018

10 9 8 7 6 5 4 3 2 1

FRI

Design by Cerise Steel
Text set in Sentinel

TO HERVÉ
AND
OUR LIGHT,
LUCIE LEE

FASHIONOPOLIS

The SECRETS Behind
the Clothes We Wear

PART ONE

Actress Cate Blanchett wearing a Mary Katrantzou gown at the 71st Cannes Film Festival.
© 2018 by George Pimentel/Getty Images.

ONE

READY TO WEAR

Walk into a fast-fashion store—a Zara, an H&M, an Urban Outfitters, a Gap—and what do you see? A cool space with cool music and cool sales assistants who are eager to help you. But most of all you will see racks and racks of cool clothes. Dresses, shirts, pants, jeans. All affordable—even cheap.

What you don't see is how these clothes were made. Where they are made. Who makes them. You don't know what the factory looks like. Is it clean and safe? Or a dirty, illegal, falling-down building, known as a sweatshop?

You don't know how the cotton was grown. Or how the sheep that were raised for the wool were treated. Or what it takes to make synthetic fabrics—meaning non-natural fabrics—such as polyester, nylon, spandex, or rayon. What *is* rayon anyway?

And you don't see where all those cool design ideas came from.

What I'm about to lay out for you here are the basics of mass production, or the "supply chain": the system of companies and people making and delivering an item. For a T-shirt, the supply chain begins with the cotton farmer, followed by the mill where the cotton is spun, the dye house where it is dyed, and the factory where it is sewn.

And while I'll be explaining how clothes are made, I could be talking about anything that is manufactured—from toys to electronics. I'll show how the system has been corrupted by greed, and how that greed has hurt people and the planet. I will spotlight some heroes who have fought against this dark system, and have come up with a cleaner, safer, more honest way of making and selling clothing. And I'll show you some of the amazing inventions that can take it all forward in a better way.

Let's start by looking at how the fashion business is structured.

Picture a pyramid.

In the small triangle at the top are one-of-a-kind, made-to-measure clothes for elite customers. For women, it's known as haute couture (pronounced "oat co-CHURE"), a French term that translates to "high sewing." For men, it's bespoke ("bee-SPOKE") tailoring. These clothes are primarily sewn by hand, and require several fittings on the customer. For women, fittings are usually done in

Paris, since that's where most haute couture houses are based. For men, it's traditionally in London—the best tailor shops have long been located on a street named Savile Row. Haute couture prices are about the same as for cars: $25,000 and up for a suit or dress, and $100,000 or more for an evening gown. Bespoke suits cost around $6,000, and easily can run up to $10,000, depending on the choice of fabric.

Haute couture designers, known as couturiers ("coo-TUR-ee-ays"), traditionally present their new designs during fashion shows in Paris each January and July. Bespoke menswear shows are usually staged in Florence, Italy, in January and June. When actors and actresses walk the red carpets at awards shows like the Oscars and the Golden Globes, they are often wearing haute couture and bespoke creations lent to or made for them by brands to generate publicity. That's why red-carpet reporters always ask stars: "Who are you wearing?"

Haute couture and bespoke are the most creative and beautifully executed clothes in fashion, and serve as inspiration for the next level on the pyramid: ready-to-wear, the factory-made clothes you find in department stores, nice boutiques, and online. (Think of it this way: Couture and bespoke is made just for you, and requires several visits to get the fit just right. Ready-to-wear is exactly as it sounds: When you buy it in a store or online, it is ready to wear. You can put it on and walk out the door!) Ready-to-wear covers a broad range of quality—from luxury brands such as Gucci and Prada, to mall stores like Ann Taylor and Brooks Brothers. Even casual wear brands Patagonia and Levi's are, officially, ready-to-wear. Generally, ready-to-wear is well made, in good fabrics. Solid, nice-looking clothes of value. Clothes you keep and wear for a while.

The wide slice on the bottom of the pyramid is fast-fashion: cheap, trendy clothes produced in vast amounts at lightning speed, and sold in thousands of chain stores worldwide.

Fast-fashion is a new addition to the pyramid, born in the 1990s. But it has grown rapidly, and is the cause of many of the problems that plague the clothing business today.

For designs, fast-fashion companies tend to copy—or "knock off"—what they see in the ready-to-wear shows. A fast-fashion brand may tweak the outfit it copies—change the color, or fiddle with the print design—to avoid being accused of outright stealing. But it is theft, no question about it.

To make clothes that they can sell not only for a lower retail price than ready-to-wear, but an extremely low price, fast-fashion brands reduce the production cost at every turn. Production price is what the brand pays to have the garment made—and includes materials, labor, shipping. Retail price is what you pay in the store.

Fast-fashion brands squeeze production costs wherever they can. They use the cheapest fabric available—usually a synthetic, like polyester or rayon, even though those fabrics create a lot of pollution both when they're made and when they're eventually thrown away. (Most never biodegrade, or break down, in landfill.) They have the clothes sewn by workers in the world's poorest countries—places like Bangladesh, Cambodia, Myanmar, Sri Lanka, Ethiopia, and the Philippines. When I visited Bangladesh in 2018, the minimum wage for workers who make clothes, or "apparel," was $68 a month, or less than $3 a day. Generally, if a fast-fashion shirt costs $10, the person who made it was paid ten cents.

The factory owner gets paid a bit of the remaining $9.90. Shipping costs a portion of it too. There are the tariffs—taxes charged by governments on products imported, or brought in, to their countries. And there are distribution costs.

But the biggest slice of that $9.90 goes to the brand as profits, the money that the company earns after paying the costs of producing and selling an item. The profit is multiplied by a number of T-shirts made and sold—the larger the number, the larger the profit. Each year, Americans buy 3.5 *billion* T-shirts. Say about half of that

$9.90 is profit. (Though the profit percentage—called "the margin"—is probably more than half.) That means brands make more than $17 billion a year on T-shirts in the United States alone.

This is why fast-fashion brand owners are multi-millionaires, or billionaires, and are among the richest people in the world.

Now, let's look at what this pyramid gives us.

Today, fashion is a $3-trillion-a-year industry.

It produces about 100 billion items annually; we buy 80 billion. The remaining 20 billion are destroyed—usually burned or shredded.

The average garment is worn seven times before being thrown away, according to a UK study. In China, it is reportedly three times.

Roughly one out of every six people works in fashion.

The majority of factory workers are women, and 98 percent are not paid a living wage—the figure calculated by economists as the amount you need to house, feed, and clothe yourself and your family.

In 2020, six of the top fifty wealthiest people in the world owned fashion companies. The sixth-richest person in the world was Amancio Ortega, the cofounder and owner of Zara. He was worth $70 billion—a *billion* times more than what the Bangladesh workers were paid each month.

According to the World Bank, the clothing industry is responsible for 20 percent of all industrial water pollution, and 10 percent of all carbon emissions.

When you walk into a fast-fashion store, everything may *look* cool.

But in reality, it is not cool.

Not at all.

To understand how the fashion industry got to this point of outright thieving and abuse of the environment and humankind, with no consequences, I decided to follow the creation of a ready-to-wear collection, from the first ideas to the sale of finished clothes. For my study, I chose Mary Katrantzou (pronounced "ka-TRAN-zoo").

She is a Greek-born, London-based women's clothing designer who specializes in fun, colorful prints that are easy to wear. The fashion press calls her the Queen of Prints. Her company is small—she rings up about $6 million a year in sales. (In comparison, Gucci does roughly $10 billion, and Zara and H&M each pull in about $20 billion.) Despite the tiny size of her company, Katrantzou's influence is large.

I first met with Katrantzou's fabric expert, Raffaella Mandriota, a young woman from Italy. On a cold February morning in 2018, Mandriota took me to Première Vision, the world's largest textile trade show. Première Vision, or

"PV" for short, is held for three days, twice a year, in an enormous convention center outside of Paris. More than 60,000 people from 120 countries go there to shop for fabric, leather, and accessories. PV is where every major—and many a minor—fashion brand's new collection of products each season begins to take shape.

Each booth was filled with clothing racks holding hundreds of fabric samples—or "swatches"—on little hangers. Mandriota whipped through the racks, giving each swatch a proper look, if only for a tenth of a second, and a feel, to understand the texture and movement of the fabric. When she thought one might work, she pulled it and placed it on her mounting pile—or "selection"—on a table. When she finished—in ten minutes, max—a company representative wrote up the order. Mandriota does this at PV twelve to fifteen times a day. In our two ten-hour days there, she ordered at least a thousand samples.

Six weeks later, cartons filled with swatches began to arrive at Mary Katrantzou's studio in London. Katrantzou, Mandriota, and several assistants whittled the mountain of fabric down to a small hill. The collection that season would celebrate Katrantzou's tenth anniversary in business. For it, she decided to rework some of her favorite print patterns, such as images of blown-glass perfume bottles; vintage postage stamps; nature, such as insects, butterflies, and seashells; and the arts. Mandriota asked some of the textile suppliers to redesign samples she'd selected at PV in Katrantzou's new print designs.

When the final orders were delivered to Katrantzou's studio, her team used the fabrics to sew samples of her designs. For six weeks, Katrantzou conducted fittings on her longtime house model, Julia. (A house model is the person who tries on the clothes in the studio for the designer to review. The designer adjusts and pins each outfit to fit the model—thus why the practice is called a "fitting.") In late June, Katrantzou presented a selection of her more commercial designs to store owners and buyers—known as retailers—in a showroom in Paris that she rented during menswear week. (A "showroom" is exactly as it sounds: a big space, like a conference room, where the clothes are on display on racks, and the designer shows them to everyone who visits.) The retailers examined each item of this "pre-collection" thoughtfully and placed their orders.

Katrantzou saved the flashiest pieces for her "show collection," which she unveiled during London Fashion Week in September. Like haute couture and bespoke, top ready-to-wear designers present their collections in fashion shows twice a year—in February and September—in New York, London, Milan, or Paris. (Many other cities have their own local fashion weeks.)

I went to Katrantzou's show, at the Roundhouse, a

theater in London, in September 2018, and spotted a few of the materials Mandriota had selected at the PV fabric fair: the organza on which a stamp motif was printed for swishy dresses; a fine transparent plastic that Mandriota had pleated in Japan, layered over geometric dresses; a white tulle, which is a netting-like material, embroidered with wildflowers for a romantic mid-length dress.

During the show, Katrantzou's guests uploaded pictures and video clips of their favorite looks on social media platforms such as Instagram and Twitter. And design teams for fast-fashion brands immediately perused those images, noted the number of "likes," and chose which designs they would steal. As I walked out of the show, a top online retail executive mused: "I bet Topshop is already working on that butterfly print."

The fast-fashion brands would then send the copied designs to factories in Bangladesh, Cambodia, Honduras, and other countries where workers would be paid less than a living wage to make the clothes in cheap fabrics by the thousands. In a matter of weeks, the fake Katrantzous would be on sale in stores for less than one hundred dollars—a fraction of what Katrantzou's more luxurious originals would later cost.

Those fast-fashion items would be worn a few times, then thrown away. What stayed on the store rack for more than a week or two would be marked down, and marked down again. If those clothes still didn't sell, the company would shred or burn them.

This is how the fashion business has functioned for 250 years: creative theft, indifference for others, corruption, pollution.

Ever since an English entrepreneur named Richard Arkwright decided that faster was better.

The Industrial Revolution kicked off in 1771, when English businessman Richard Arkwright pulled together a bunch of other people's inventions—such as Lewis Paul's carding machine and James Hargreaves's spinning jenny—and opened the world's first water-powered textile mill, near Manchester, England. *Clack-clack-clackety-clack*, the machines roared, shaking the five-story building, cotton filaments floating through the air like snowflakes.

Desperately poor men, women, and even children flocked to Manchester from the countryside for jobs in those factories. They were low-paying jobs, but employment in factories sounded better to the people than their hard lives on farms or in slums. For the most part, they were wrong.

The machines spun the cotton into yarn, then wove the yarn into fabric. Clothes were still made by hand—by wives and mothers at home, and by local dressmakers and tailors in workshops. The sewing machine wouldn't be invented for many decades to come.

The days in the factory were long: Workers would put in thirteen hours, with two short breaks for meals; the mills stopped only for one hour a day. Everyone lived in brick row houses on the factory grounds, so they would be close to their jobs. At first, there were two hundred workers; within ten years, a thousand. With the enormous, and fast, output, cotton soon replaced wool as the most popular material for clothes. By 1790, Richard Arkwright owned nearly two hundred mills throughout Great Britain, and Manchester had become known as "Cottonopolis."

In 1810, a Boston businessman named Francis Cabot Lowell traveled to England. His mission: to steal Arkwright's manufacturing system. Lowell toured the Manchester mills, memorized the power loom mechanics, returned to Massachusetts, and reconstructed the machines. Three years later, Lowell opened the Boston Manufacturing Company on the Charles River in Waltham, Massachusetts, to spin and weave the American cotton harvested by enslaved people. American cotton came from farms, or "plantations," in the South owned by wealthy white people. Enslaved people planted the cotton, nurtured it, harvested it, and loaded it onto ships to send to the mills in Massachusetts. Like in England, the finished cloth was still cut and sewed by hand, which took time.

With the invention of the lockstitch sewing machine in the 1830s, clothes could be made faster too. But mass-manufactured apparel, as clothing is known in the fashion business, didn't really catch on with customers until the Civil War in the 1860s, when the Union and Confederate armies suddenly needed thousands of sturdy uniforms in standard sizes. Factories in the United States opened or expanded to meet the demand. The troops so liked the convenience and fit of those uniforms that, after the war, they sought out street clothes made the same way. Manufacturers began producing menswear, and then women's wear, at affordable prices—it was cheaper to make the same garment on machines by the hundreds than it was for a seamstress or tailor to hand-sew a dress or suit one at a time. These factory-made clothes were the first "ready-to-wear."

Clothing manufacturing in the United States in those early days was divided into two categories: basics, like work clothes and underwear, produced at big factories in Massachusetts and Pennsylvania; and stylish, high-quality "fashion" made in smaller amounts in workshops on New York City's Lower East Side.

Why New York? It was America's busiest port, where wool and silk arrived from Europe and Asia. It was the financial center, with bankers eager to put money into the booming fashion industry. And it was the country's main immigration point. Thousands of European immigrants arrived by ship every week, looking for jobs. The easiest job to land in New York was sewing clothes—there was a demand in garment factories, and many immigrants knew how to sew since tailoring and dressmaking were still valued skills in Europe. In the late nineteenth century, more than half of the people living on New York's Lower East Side worked in clothing production. Most of what they made was inspired by—or copied from—Paris couture designs. The pyramid model was born.

As demand grew for mass-produced fashion, so did the need for new factories. They were built in a section of Midtown Manhattan that became known as the Garment District. In the center was the newly opened railway hub, Pennsylvania Station. This allowed for out-of-town retailers to arrive by train and visit showrooms and factories easily. In 1931, the New York Garment District had more apparel factories than anywhere else in the world.

In the late 1950s, the manufacturing of basic clothing, such as T-shirts, jeans, underwear, and socks, began to leave New York City, and move to Upstate New York, Pennsylvania, and Chicago. The reason? Cost. It was cheaper to build factories, and to live, in those places.

Company owners could invest less in construction, and pay workers less, and pocket more profits.

The factories that stayed in the city switched their focus to higher-quality fashion. Midtown workers wheeled racks of finished clothes down city sidewalks to the showrooms and shipping warehouses. In 1973, four hundred thousand people worked in the Garment District. In all, 70 percent of the clothing that Americans bought in 1980 was made in the United States.

Then politicians stepped in, and everything changed.

Tariffs (pronounced "TARE-iffs") are taxes charged by a government on items that are imported to or exported from a country. The term comes from the Italian word *tariffa*, which means "list of prices." When something is made overseas, and it is brought (or imported) into the country, customs officials charge a tariff on it, like sales tax. Sometimes the exporter pays. Sometimes the importer pays. Sometimes they both pay. The amount of the tariff is set by laws and treaties. Tariffs bring a lot of money into the national treasury.

Tariffs are also a form of protectionism—the practice of protecting a country's businesses from foreign competition. Let's use a T-shirt as an example, with imaginary prices. A T-shirt made in the USA might cost $20 to produce. A T-shirt made in Mexico might cost $10 to produce. So as a brand, you'd say, hmm . . . then let's produce *all* of our T-shirts in Mexico. It's half the cost! But then US customs officials place a big tariff on the T-shirt—say, $15. So now the Mexico-made T-shirt costs $25 to produce and sell in the US market. You think: "Okay, then let's produce all of our T-shirts in the United States. In the end, it's cheaper to produce here than in Mexico." The tariff protected the American factory, and its workers. That's the essence of protectionism.

The opposite of protectionism is "free trade": a system in which goods can come and go from countries without costly tariffs, quotas, or other sorts of legal restrictions. This means that that $10 T-shirt produced in Mexico could be shipped to the United States freely, and be sold at the same retail price in a store as the $20 US-made T-shirt. The brand would pocket that $10 difference in production costs as part of the profit. The brand also doesn't have to worry about other costs of running a factory, known as "overhead," such as factory upkeep, or workers' salaries, paid vacation time, paid parental leave, or health insurance. Understandably, businesses like free trade: They rake in more profits with a lot less responsibility.

After World War II, several trade deals were put in place to help the devastated countries get back on track. Factories and homes had been destroyed by bombs, and needed to be rebuilt. There were few jobs of any sort, and no one had any money to buy things. All in all, a big mess. The trade deals were put in place to clean up some of that mess. Once factories were up and running again, making products to be sold around the world, the United States reduced or eliminated tariffs on the items imported from those countries. Charging less fees and taxes on items gave the factories, and companies, a financial lift.

Some of the trade deals were with Japan, to bolster its cotton industry. The cut in tariffs allowed the companies—and the country's economy—to get strong again. There were similar trade deals with countries throughout Asia, and they were successful too, helping the countries rebound from such difficult times. Soon, textile and clothing manufacturing was so strong in Japan, South Korea, Hong Kong, Singapore, and Taiwan, the countries became known as the "Asian Tigers."

Some American clothing brands began to move—or "outsource"—their production to factories in these countries. Usually the orders were for basics, such as socks, T-shirts, and underwear—things that are easy to make and produced in large amounts. The hourly wage workers were paid was so low that, even with the cost of shipping and the tariffs, it was much cheaper to produce in these overseas lands than it was in the United States. By the mid-1970s, Hong Kong had become the world's largest apparel exporter.

In 1980, former California governor Ronald Reagan decided to run as the Republican candidate for president of the United States. During his campaign kickoff speech, he suggested that Canada, Mexico, and the United States open their borders to free trade, meaning products moving freely among the three countries without import tariffs. He won the election, and launched what is now known as the Reagan Revolution—an economic plan that was heavy on free trade. Often apparel deals were complicated, but they encouraged American companies to produce offshore.

The resulting job losses in American factories so worried US workers that groups of them, called unions, successfully lobbied Congress to officially name December 1986 "Made in America Month." The joint resolution passed by Congress stressed "the importance of buying American" and warned that the flood of imports could permanently damage the country's fashion industry.

American apparel manufacturers also came up with a new, more cost-efficient way to produce clothing: "quick response," or "QR." Usually, clothing collections were designed a year in advance—with the designers *guessing* what might be hot—and if the clothes didn't sell, they were destroyed. With QR, brands and retailers could test looks with potential shoppers *before* putting the clothes into production. Orders would be smaller and more often. If sales were good, the brands would respond quickly and order up more. QR would give customers what they wanted, where they wanted it, when they wanted it. There would be fewer leftovers and less waste, which would save companies money. And saving money in costs meant more profits, making brand owners richer.

There was one big problem: Any factory anywhere could use QR to make their system run better. Even America's foreign competitors—like the businessman Amancio Ortega Gaona, the owner of a small Spanish fashion company called Zara.

Zara began as a single shop in La Coruña, a town in northwest Spain. It was opened in 1975 by longtime apparel manufacturer Amancio Ortega Gaona and his then-wife, Rosalía Mera. Originally, they called it Zorba, after the novel *Zorba the Greek*. When they discovered there was already a café Zorba in La Coruña, they changed the name to Zara.

For its clothes, Ortega followed the old-school ready-to-wear model—seasonal collections of trendy clothes inspired by haute couture and high fashion. Everything was produced in Spain. It worked well—one store grew to eighty-five in Spain by 1989. And Ortega made a good living. But he wanted more.

QR was the key. If Ortega merged QR's speedy production practices with retailing, he could rev up *everything*: trends, sales, and profits. Since he made the clothes in Spain and sold them in Spain, with QR, he could get them to stores quickly, sell them quickly, restock quickly. Normally, the fashion cycle was divided into two seasons: fall-winter, and spring-summer. Store deliveries were twice a year—in late winter for spring-summer, and in late summer for fall-winter. Sometimes, there'd be mid-season deliveries, or "drops," in May for summer and in November for the holidays.

Ortega ignored all that. He dropped new styles on Zara sales floors constantly. The regular update pulled customers into Zara stores four times more often than at competitors' stores. And since customers went more often, they bought more clothes. As sales rose, Ortega began to outsource production across the Mediterranean Sea, in Morocco, where labor costs were lower than in Spain. With the factories so near, he could still guarantee rapid delivery.

Soon, Gap, Urban Outfitters, H&M, and Benetton followed Ortega's lead—they sped up their manufacturing, produced in countries with cheap labor, and sold clothes at low prices as quickly as possible. The press dubbed this new system "fast-fashion" because it followed the same rhythm of production and consumption as fast food.

Ten years after Ronald Reagan introduced the idea of unifying the United States, Canada, and Mexico as a "common market," Congress passed the North American Free Trade Agreement (NAFTA), a free trade agreement with the United States, Canada, and Mexico. NAFTA would remove most tariffs on goods moving between the three countries.

NAFTA supporters argued that, without tariffs, goods would cost less. The lower prices would encourage people in Mexico, Canada, and the United States to shop more, and buy more. That would push US factories to produce more, and, to keep up, they'd have to hire more people. "NAFTA means jobs, American jobs, and good-paying American jobs," President Bill Clinton said.

Not everyone agreed. Texan billionaire businessman Ross Perot, who ran for president as an independent against Democratic candidate Bill Clinton and Republican candidate George H. W. Bush in 1992, predicted that NAFTA would cause American companies to close factories in the United States and move production—with "a giant sucking sound"—to Mexico, where *everything*—factories, workers, materials—was a fraction of the cost. And that is exactly what happened. By 2006, NAFTA was responsible for the loss of at least one million jobs in the United States, a good many of them in clothing and fabric production.

This is when globalization—the process of spreading production, technology, and information around the world—took off. Apparel manufacturing moved from Europe and the United States to Central America, China, Southeast Asia, Africa, Turkey, India, and Pakistan. Fabric would be woven and dyed in one place, cut in another, sewed in a third, with zippers and buttons attached in a fourth. And finishing touches, like embroidery or denim distressing (when workers hand sand edges and knees of jeans to give them a worn look), were done in yet another land. Nearly every step was—and is—contracted to independent factories; few fashion companies own the factories where their clothes are produced.

Brands were producing more and more clothes: Between 2000 and 2014, the number doubled to 100 billion items annually—or fourteen new pieces of clothing per person per year for every person on the planet. Zara began putting new styles in its stores *every* week. Sales rocketed. Shoppers were going to most fast-fashion brands' boutiques four times a year; for Zara, they went seventeen.

Between 2000 and 2014, the price of most goods—everything from bread to cell phones—increased by about 50 percent. If something cost $100 in 2000, it cost $150 in 2014. But, thanks to the cost-cutting all along the fashion supply chain, clothing prices actually *dropped*.

So, consumers bought *more* clothes. Wore them less. Grew bored with them faster. And got rid of them faster.

"Throwaway clothes" became normal.

Garment worker Shila Begum at Rana Plaza in Bangladesh.
© 2018 by Clara Vannucci.

TWO

THE PRICE OF FURIOUS FASHION

Los Angeles is known as the movie capital of the world, with Hollywood premieres, the Oscar Awards, glamour and glitz.

But what you probably don't know is that it's also the largest fashion manufacturing center in America. Thousands of factories in and around Los Angeles produce T-shirts, jeans—all sorts of clothes. Many of these manufacturers are downtown. And many are sweatshops—illegal, run-down factories where workers are treated badly and earn far below the legal minimum wage, which is the lowest amount the government says companies can pay workers.

Sweatshops were invented in the nineteenth century in New York. To save money, factory owners would set up workshops in tiny apartments—an arrangement called "kitchen and bedroom" shops. Up to thirty people would be squeezed into this small space, with worktables arranged too tightly to walk past. Sewing machines clattered in the center of the front room. The *average* workweek was eighty-four hours—or twelve hours a day, seven days a week.

The bosses were tyrants who would "sweat" their employees—forcing longer hours for less money—thus the term *sweatshop*.

Though sweatshops are now officially illegal in the United States, they still exist—mostly in Los Angeles and New York. The bosses hire undocumented immigrants, often from Mexico or Central America. Undocumented immigrants enter the country without the proper paperwork, such as a temporary work visa, or they stay after the visa has expired. Without US citizenship or valid visas, it's difficult for these immigrants to find jobs with law-abiding companies. But sweatshop owners will hire them. Since these jobs are "underground"—meaning everything is done in hiding, and the government knows nothing about it—the factory owners pay the workers far less than the legal minimum wage.

Sweatshops are usually located in old, tired buildings that are dangerous and dirty, and do not meet the government's safety regulations or health rules. Because the buildings are in such bad shape, the rent is cheap. This allows the factory owner to make more money—more profit.

On a hot September morning, I visited one of these sweatshops, in the Bendix Building, a shabby, eleven-story office tower that was built in the 1920s, in what is now known as LA's Fashion District.

The Fashion District is a neighborhood a few blocks away from downtown Los Angeles's bustling business center. In the Fashion District, there are outdoor clothing markets and low-price stores, as well as legitimate factories and illegal sweatshops.

I toured the Bendix Building with Mariela "Mar" Martinez, an organizer for the Garment Worker Center, a nonprofit workers' rights organization that fights to close LA's sweatshops and improve job conditions for garment workers.

We took the elevator to the top floor and walked down the hallway. Some of the sweatshop doors were slightly open, and I was able to peek inside. I saw workers hunched over machines in badly lit rooms, sewing clothes. The floors were cluttered with piles of fabric. Thread, scraps, and dust bunnies were everywhere.

Suddenly, doors began to slam shut, one after the other. *Boom! Boom! Boom!*

"Wow, that was quick," Martinez said. Someone had recognized her and alerted the neighbors, which were also sweatshops. We went down to the eighth floor; the sweatshop doors were already closed and locked. The tip-off went building-wide.

We took the elevator back to the lobby and walked

across the street to the Allied Crafts Building, another crummy downtown tower that houses sweatshops. Martinez explained that most LA sweatshop workers are Latino, and most sweatshop owners are Korean. We climbed the stairs to the third floor. Windowpanes were broken. A man—a manager, perhaps—sat on a step of the rusty fire escape, smoking. "Would you go down this?" Martinez asked me, pointing to the fire escape. With skinny cables and hundred-year-old wall fasteners, it appeared it would collapse under the weight of more than a couple of people.

And once you got down to the second floor—where it stopped—you'd have to jump into a dumpster.

So, no, it didn't look like a good escape route if there was a fire. In fact, it seemed really dangerous.

"I call this the white noise of Los Angeles," Martinez said as we made our way back to the street. "No one sees it, or acknowledges it, but it's here."

Fashion manufacturing began in Los Angeles in the early twentieth century, when local knitting mills started making swimwear. The industry continued to grow over the decades, expanding into colorful casual wear known as the "California Look."

When Congress passed NAFTA in the early 1990s,

factories in the New York Garment District began to close and clothing production moved offshore to cheaper markets, like Mexico. But garment manufacturing remained in Los Angeles, because factory rent was cheaper than in New York, and so was labor: There were tens of thousands of immigrants from Mexico and Latin America looking for work.

In 2017, Martinez estimated there were 45,000 workers producing clothing in Los Angeles. About half were legal immigrants, and were paid at least the California minimum wage, which was then $10.50 an hour.

The other half—about 22,000 workers—were undocumented, sewing clothes for US-based brands in illegal sweatshops for as little as $4 an hour. Unlike documented workers in legal factories, sweatshop workers are not paid for overtime, which is extra work outside of regular hours. They also do not receive benefits such as health insurance, paid vacation, sick leave, or parental leave. They work in dirty, unsafe conditions. All of these illegal practices save *a lot* of money in production costs. Therefore, the brands who hire illegal workshops make much bigger profits.

Because the clothes are made in Los Angeles, the brands are allowed to print *Made in the USA* on the labels. This happens even when the clothes are made in sweatshops. Labels only indicate the location, and the materials used; it doesn't say *how* the clothes were made. When clothes have the label *Made in the USA,* consumers believe that those items were produced in safe, clean factories, by workers who were well paid and received basic benefits. And consumers believe when they buy those clothes, they are making a patriotic choice—supporting fellow Americans, and supporting the American economy. But the clothes could have been—and often are—manufactured in sweatshops like the ones I saw with Mar Martinez in Los Angeles. By making clothes in sweatshops and putting a *Made in the USA* label on them, brands are tricking consumers. And brands are earning a greater profit by taking advantage of the poor and underprivileged. Just like Richard Arkwright did 250 years ago.

That's what pulled Martinez into the fight. A young woman in her twenties, she grew up a few miles from the Garment Worker Center, in South Central LA. Her parents worked in the city's legitimate garment industry. She became a human rights activist while in high school and carried on while a student at Brown University, in Rhode Island. After she graduated, she returned to Los Angeles and joined the Garment Worker Center as its organizing coordinator.

Two afternoons a week, she meets with workers in the center's windowless offices in a two-story building on Los Angeles Street and listens to their complaints. Most common is "wage theft": when bosses pay workers much less than the state or federal minimum wage. If the minimum wage is $10 an hour, and the workers are paid $4 an hour, the sweatshop is stealing $6 an hour from the workers. That is wage theft.

Usually, Martinez will contact the sweatshop owner or manager and try to get money for the workers. If the case is especially bad, she'll turn it over to government officials, who will launch an investigation. Sometimes, the government officials, with the help of law enforcement, will raid the sweatshop and shut it down. According to a study by the UCLA Labor Center, released in 2016, brands allegedly producing in Los Angeles sweatshops included Forever 21, Wet Seal, Papaya, and Charlotte Russe. When caught, the brands usually say they had no idea their "approved" factories were giving the work—or "subcontracting"—to sweatshops. "[Brands] wash their hands of the problem," Martinez said. "Nobody cares."

For his mills to succeed, Richard Arkwright needed cotton. Lots of it. And in the late eighteenth and early nineteenth centuries, the British Empire had a vast network of shipping trade routes to get that cotton to Manchester. The cotton was grown in the British colonies of America and the West Indies in the Caribbean, and it was shipped to England as part of the triangular trading system known as the transatlantic slave trade.

Slave traders captured people in Europe's African colonies and sold them to plantation owners in America and the Caribbean Islands as laborers. Enslaved people planted and nurtured the cotton. Enslaved people harvested the cotton. Enslaved people loaded the cotton onto ships headed for Arkwright's factories in England. As the nineteenth-century German philosopher Karl Marx later observed: "Without slavery, there would be no cotton. Without cotton, there would be no modern industry."

To spin the cotton, Arkwright needed armies of workers. Hundreds of poor people arrived from the countryside. Most were women; men remained on the farm to tend the fields. Before Arkwright, women stayed at home and raised children; he turned women into money earners. He hired their children too, and paid them even less than the adults.

Workers stood for hours in uncomfortable positions, handling heavy machinery, which caused terrible injuries: deformed legs and pelvises; lost fingers, hands, or arms. The fibrous dust they inhaled on the plant floor caused respiratory infections, asthma, and tuberculosis.

Half of the workers were children. Starting age was usually eight or nine. The hours were long, and the children were always exhausted. The endless hours Cottonopolis factory children spent on their feet stunted their growth and caused ailments such as chronic back pain, varicose veins, and large, infected ulcers on their legs. Many were injured or killed by the machines. Sometimes, child workers tried to escape. If they were caught, they'd be beaten. The tales in former factory boy Robert Blincoe's 1828 memoir were so scary, the book is believed to have inspired English author Charles Dickens to write *Oliver Twist*.

In the 1840s, Friedrich Engels, the twenty-two-year-old son of a German textile mill owner, was sent by his father to Manchester to learn the business. Engels was so appalled by what he saw in the factories that he wrote a book in 1845 called *The Condition of the Working Class in England*. In the book, Engels said that mill workers were "robbed of all humanity" and trapped in unimaginable poverty. Factory work, Engels wrote, was a new mode of enslavement.

Public outrage eventually pushed the British government to pass a series of laws regulating factory conditions and wages, including reducing or eliminating child labor. But the new regulations were ignored since, as Engels pointed out, the fines were small compared to "the certain profits" the factory owners earned. And even with those regulations to protect factory workers in England, the British government didn't outlaw importing the cotton that was grown and harvested by enslaved people across the Atlantic.

When the garment industry moved to America in the nineteenth century, the labor abuses followed. In New York City's sweatshops, tailors sat on stools along the walls of the tiny rooms, sewing. Some sat on the floor to do their work, surrounded by bits of thread, cloth, and pins. Pressers—the people who ironed the clothes—were in the kitchen, heating the irons on the stove next to where the staff meal was simmering. On occasion, an iron would fall into the soup, infuriating the owner's wife, who did the cooking. Children slept on piles of finished clothes, and everything was covered with dirt. Tuberculosis, a deadly lung disease, was so common in these ateliers, it was nicknamed "the tailor's disease."

Life as it was in a Lower Manhattan garment workshop can be viewed today at the Tenement Museum, a town house at 97 Orchard Street that had been boarded up for more than half a century, its interiors preserved like a time capsule. Built when Abraham Lincoln was president, the narrow, five-story brownstone was divided into twenty-two tiny apartments—most of the rooms are the size of a walk-in closet, and all are dark and dingy. At first, there were only outhouses, well water, and gas lighting; later, indoor plumbing and electricity were installed.

There were twenty-three similar factories on the same block.

In the 1890s, worker activist Florence "Pig" Kelley set out to abolish sweatshops in the United States. Kelley argued that modern mechanization and streamlined distribution, rather than low wages, were the most effective ways to reduce production costs. Basically: Run your business better, and more efficiently, and you'll make more in profits.

In fact, Kelley believed that the sweatshop system actually *increased* costs, because it discouraged owners from investing in new, more efficient machinery. She called for boycotts, stating: "If the people would notify [Chicago department store retailer] Marshall Field . . . and others that they would buy from them no clothing made in sweatshops, the evil would be stopped."

Kelley was the first general secretary of the National Consumers League, a nationwide nonprofit founded in 1899 to inform consumers about business corruption and worker abuse. One of the league's first projects was the "white label"—a garment tag that confirmed the manufacturer had respected state employment and safety laws. The white label encouraged shoppers to think ethically about their purchases.

Sadly, that wasn't enough to make American garment factories safe. In 1911, the Triangle Shirtwaist Factory in downtown New York City caught on fire. Workers ran onto the rickety fire escape, and it collapsed. Dozens of workers jumped from windows and the roof. In all, 146 employees died—123 women and 23 men. It was New York City's worst workplace disaster until the terrorist attacks of September 11, 2001.

After the Triangle Shirtwaist Factory fire, the public demanded change. No more sweatshops. No more worker abuse. Frances Perkins, dynamic advocate for worker rights, would lead the fight.

Perkins had served as the executive secretary of the New York City Consumers League, where she worked with Florence Kelley. After the Triangle Shirtwaist fire, she joined New York State's Industrial Commission, and fought to make factories safer. In the 1930s, President Franklin D. Roosevelt named Perkins the secretary of labor, the country's first female cabinet member. During her twelve years in the job—the longest anyone has held that post—many landmark acts were passed and agencies were created, including the Public Works Administration; the Social Security Act, which established unemployment, welfare, and retirement benefits; and the Fair Labor Standards Act (FLSA), which set the country's first minimum wage, guaranteed overtime payment, banned child labor, and instituted the forty-hour workweek.

With the FLSA, American manufacturing cleaned up

and moved into its golden age. And so it remained, until NAFTA went into effect in the early 1990s, and clothing production moved offshore. In developing countries, where the economy isn't as strong as it is in the United States and a great number of citizens live in poverty, there were and are fewer safety and labor laws, and even less enforcement of the ones that do exist. American companies began manufacturing clothing in many of those countries, such as Mexico, Honduras, and Bangladesh, and the old-style sweatshop system came roaring back to life.

This is why, within six months of Congress passing NAFTA in 1993, the House Subcommittee on Labor Management found itself holding hearings on worker abuses in a Honduran factory where the American women's wear brand Leslie Fay produced its clothes. Established in 1947 by Fred Pomerantz, an apparel executive who had worked in Manhattan's Garment District from age eleven, Leslie Fay was known for its pretty dresses, sewed by union workers in Wilkes-Barre, Pennsylvania. (A union is a professional association that fights for labor rights on behalf of its members—in this case, factory workers.)

When Fred retired in 1982, his middle-aged son, John Pomerantz, who had worked for Leslie Fay for decades, took over the company. In 1993, Leslie Fay had financial troubles and filed for bankruptcy. Pomerantz had long resisted outsourcing, because he believed it was good business, as well as patriotic, to produce in America.

With the bankruptcy, he changed his mind. He moved Leslie Fay production to Honduras. And soon it became apparent that, like so many other American fashion companies that were manufacturing offshore, Leslie Fay's executives had no idea how the brand's clothes were made.

They learned, to their embarrassment, from witnesses during the congressional hearings. Dorka Nohemi Diaz Lopez, a twenty-year-old Honduran who sewed Leslie Fay dresses and blouses, testified that girls as young as thirteen were on the factory floor, earning 40 to 50 cents an hour; Leslie Fay's US-based workers were paid $7.80 an hour. The girls worked twelve-hour shifts or longer. Temperatures were often more than 100 degrees Fahrenheit, and there wasn't clean drinking water. "The doors are locked," Lopez said, "and you can't get out until they let you."

Many American apparel companies, including J.Crew, Eddie Bauer, and Levi Strauss, faced similar charges. In response, some brands started drafting "codes of conduct": a list of rules that a company expects its suppliers to respect. To enforce the codes, brands hired independent monitors to conduct inspections. But the voluntary inspection system was corrupt. Inspectors announced their visits in advance, so factories could be cleaned and workers told what to say. Bribery was common. And scandals kept surfacing.

In 2003, American rap stars Sean "P-Diddy" Combs and Jay-Z were caught up in one: Clothes for their hip-hop fashion brands Sean John and Rocawear were found to be made in Honduran sweatshops. At a Senate committee hearing in November 2003, Lydda Eli Gonzalez, a nineteen-year-old Honduran garment worker, recalled the horrors she had experienced at a factory where Sean John and Rocawear were produced.

The factory was surrounded by a towering wall and the entrance had a locked metal gate with guards. Official hours were 7:00 a.m. to 4:45 p.m.—at 75 to 98 cents an hour—but there was mandatory unpaid overtime. The Sean John shirts sold for $40 apiece at American department stores such as Bloomingdale's. The factory produced more than a thousand shirts each day. "Just one shirt would pay more than my wage for a week," Gonzalez testified.

Supervisors would "stand over us shouting and cursing at us to go faster [and calling] us filthy names," she said. The temperature rose so high, workers were "sweating all day." Fabric fibers and dust turned their hair "white or red or whatever the color of the shirts we are working on." The drinking water was dirty. Workers were forbidden to speak. They could only use the bathroom once in the morning and once in the afternoon; usually, there was no toilet paper or soap. Everyone was frisked upon entering the factory each day, and anything found, including candy or lipstick, was taken away. They were searched again when they went home.

Combs understood this news could ruin his brand and promptly stepped in. Within ten weeks, it was announced that the production bosses had been fired; overtime was now voluntary and paid; locks had been taken off bathrooms; there was air-conditioning and clean water.

Nevertheless, pay remained hopelessly low. "Really, you work just to eat. It's impossible to save. You can't buy anything. It's just to survive," Gonzalez told the Senate committee. "I'm no better off than I was two or three years ago. We are in a trap."

No place is the trap more dangerous than the People's Republic of Bangladesh, a developing country located between India and Myanmar in southeast Asia. In 2019, Bangladesh had 168 million citizens. One-fourth of them lived below the poverty line. In 2018, 4 million workers made more than $30 billion worth of clothes for export, ranking Bangladesh the number two apparel producer, after China/Hong Kong. "Our economy is dependent on it," Siddiqur Rahman, president of the Bangladesh Garment Manufacturers and Exporters Association in 2018, told me then.

Bangladesh began producing clothes in the 1970s, after the country's war of independence from Pakistan. As with every new garment industry center before it, poor young women went—or were sent by their families—to the city for factory jobs. Bangladesh became the cheapest place to produce apparel—a new Manchester.

Suppliers built shoddy factories by the thousands, often without such safety basics as fire exits. But, like in Honduras, the factories always had strict security, to ensure workers couldn't try to steal product. Because Bangladesh factories were so far from the United States and Europe, most brand executives and customers had no idea how grim these factories were—and are.

Those who do understand are the people who work for non-governmental organizations (NGOs)—independent associations that tackle social and environmental issues. One such NGO is the International Labor Rights Forum (ILRF), a nonprofit human rights organization in Washington, DC, run by a longtime worker rights advocate named Judy Gearhart. The ILRF is "dedicated to achieving dignity and justice for workers worldwide."

It's not an easy assignment.

Between 2006 and 2012, more than five hundred

Bangladeshi garment workers died in factory fires. One of the worst was in December 2010, when the ten-story That's It Sportswear garment factory, which produced clothes for Gap, Tommy Hilfiger, and Kohl's, went up in flames. The factory had just passed inspection by representatives of Gap. Yet, the fire exits were locked, which is in violation of brand safety codes, like Gap's. Because the workers could not escape the fire, more than one hundred were injured, and twenty-nine died.

After the fire, worker unions and NGOs—including the ILRF—sat down with brands to discuss factory safety. They came up with a plan called the Bangladesh Fire and Building Safety Agreement, which laid out how to improve conditions—like no more locked fire exits, better sprinkler systems, evacuation training, safe electrical wiring. All brands had to do was sign the agreement, and the reforms and repairs would happen.

But reforms and repairs cost money, which means less profits.

No brand signed the agreement.

In winter of 2012, ABC News in New York broadcast a story on television about the That's It Sportswear fire. For the story, the reporters questioned the designer Tommy Hilfiger on why he was producing in such an unsafe factory. He insisted such practices would change. Within days, PVH Corp., the corporation that owns Tommy Hilfiger, signed the Bangladesh Fire and Building

Safety Agreement. Six months later, the German retail chain Tchibo also signed. But no one else did, and the agreement couldn't go into effect until four companies signed.

On a November evening that year, twenty-three-year-old Sumi Abedin was sitting at her sewing machine on the fourth floor of the nine-story Tazreen Fashion factory when, she recalled, "a man came up and shouted that there was a fire."

Her manager and supervisor insisted everything was fine.

"There is no fire, just go back and keep working," they told the workers, and locked the door.

Fire alarms sounded.

"After five to seven minutes, I smelled smoke," Abedin remembered. "I ran to the doors, the stairs, and found that [they were] padlocked." She managed to get to the second floor, but that was it. The staircase was "blocked by the fire."

More than 1,100 workers were trapped inside. They tried to remove security bars from windows. One succeeded. He jumped. Then another jumped.

"Then I jumped," Abedin said. She broke her arm and foot.

In all, more than 200 were injured, and at least 117 died. It was the worst apparel industry accident since the Triangle Shirtwaist Factory fire a century earlier.

Investigators later found labels, clothing, and paperwork proving Sears, Walmart, and Disney had produced there. All three claimed Tazreen was not an authorized supplier.

Remarkably, even after the fire, which made the news around the world, brands still didn't sign the Bangladesh Fire and Building Safety Agreement.

That made shady garment factory owners like Sohel Rana feel all-powerful.

Sohel Rana was a corrupt Bangladeshi businessman in his mid-thirties who owned a small patch of land in Savar, a town outside of Dhaka. With the help of his armed guards, Rana stole the property next to his from a former business partner. He took ownership of another with fake paperwork. Then in 2006, on that big, empty lot, he constructed Rana Plaza, a six-story building housing garment factories, shops, and a bank. The building rose fast and cheap, without following safety codes. In 2011, Rana built two more floors. Locals believe he got the permit by bribing government officials.

On the morning of April 23, 2013, workers at the five factories in Rana Plaza were busily sewing clothes when an explosion shook the building and cracked a second-floor wall. "The crack was so huge, I could put my hand in it," Shila Begum, a young woman who worked as a sewing machine operator for Ether Tex Ltd., on the fifth floor, remembered five years later. Terrified employees poured into the street. Management called an engineer to come look at the damage. The engineer wanted to condemn the building immediately. Sohel Rana, who was at Rana Plaza that day, refused. "The plaster on the wall is broken, nothing more," he reportedly said. "It is not a problem."

Everyone was sent home but ordered to return the next morning. Around 8:00 a.m. the following day, Mahmudul Hassan Hridoy heard a knock on his front door. It was his boss and neighbor, reminding him that they were expected at work. Hridoy, a good-natured twenty-seven-year-old, was in fine form: He had just married his sweetheart that weekend, and two weeks earlier, he had quit his job as a nursery school teacher for the better paying job as a quality inspector for New Wave Style Ltd., a workshop at Rana Plaza. As he was good at math, the company said he would rise to a better job quickly.

"That's why I joined Rana Plaza," he told me over lunch at the KFC in Savar in 2018.

He listened to his boss and went to work, as did everybody else, including Shila Begum. "I was really in a panic," she recalled as we spoke on a Savar sidewalk under the hot afternoon sun in 2018. They all showed up, she said, because if they didn't, they feared they would not be paid at the end of the month. Bangladesh's minimum wage was $38 a month then—or one-third of a living wage, which economists calculate is the amount needed to cover essential needs such as housing, food, and clothing. (In January 2019, it was raised to $95 a month, which is still half a living wage.)

"I was minding my own business, making blue jeans like you are wearing, for a French brand, when the power went out," she told me. "A couple of minutes later, the generators started." As the engines rumbled, the building began to shake. And then, she said: "It went down. The concrete ceiling fell on my hand and my hair was caught in the sewing machine. After a lot of struggle, I untangled my hair, but I could not free my hand." Sixteen hours later, she was rescued. Her hand was permanently damaged and she must always wear a cast.

Hridoy was inspecting jeans on the seventh floor when everything went dark and silent. The generators started, he recalled, "and it felt like the floor under my feet was moving. Then it was disappearing." When he opened his eyes in the rubble, he realized he was pinned under a concrete pillar. As he told me this story, he began to cry. "Those memories still haunt me," he said.

With 1,134 dead and 2,500 injured, Rana Plaza was the deadliest garment factory accident in history. "I lost all of my friends," Begum said. "Many were never found."

- - -

Most brands said nothing. To figure out which brands did produce there, teams of researchers spent months digging through the rubble looking for labels, and scanning databases for information. They found some, and presented the evidence to brands that had clothes made there. Walmart claimed its orders had been subcontracted without company authorization. Carrefour of France denied producing there. JCPenney and Lee Cooper/Iconix didn't respond.

Once it became clear that more than a dozen US and European brands had clothes made at Rana Plaza, most of those companies did not pay money to survivors or victims' families for injury and loss. As there were no worker rights agreements in place, the brands were not obligated to pay.

But news stories recounting the horrific tragedy did make brands worry about their public image. The double whammy of Tazreen and Rana Plaza was too much. They had to do something. Then they remembered the Bangladesh Fire and Building Safety Agreement, which they had ignored for two years.

Within six weeks, forty-three companies, including Primark, Inditex (which owns Zara), Abercrombie & Fitch, Benetton, and H&M had signed the agreement, which had been renamed the Accord on Fire and Building

Safety. By October, there were two hundred members, among them Fast Retailing (owner of Uniqlo) and American Eagle.

A slew of other brands—mostly American—did not sign. They didn't like the fact that they would be *legally bound* to fixing factories. Instead, they came up with their own agreement, called the Alliance for Bangladesh Worker Safety, which laid out *voluntary* reforms. Among those who signed the Alliance: Gap, Target, Hudson's Bay Company (owners of Saks Fifth Avenue), and VF Corporation (owners of Lee Jeans, Wrangler, The North Face, and Timberland). It was seen as a far weaker agreement. For decades, such reforms had been voluntary, and as Tazreen and Rana Plaza proved, voluntary reforms didn't work.

Tazreen's owner, Delwar Hossain, was eventually arrested and charged with culpable homicide, meaning he knew that the factory's dangerous conditions would likely cause death.

In 2016, Sohel Rana and seventeen others, including his parents, Rana Plaza's engineer, Savar's mayor, three government inspectors, and its town planner, were charged with various crimes, including homicide. A year later, Rana was sentenced to three years in prison for not revealing the true amount of his personal fortune to the Anti-Corruption Commission.

All this happened because "the industry is obsessed with quarterly returns," meaning companies only believe they are successful if they rake in greater profits *every three months*, said Mark Anner, director of Penn State's Center for Global Workers' Rights. Those profits go to the shareholders—the people who own a portion of the company. "How do you develop a long-term vision if, every three months, shareholders demand more profits or threaten to pull out" their financial support of the company? "How does this affect workers?"

Or Bangladesh as a whole?

"If the workers made a decent wage, the economy would grow, because they could afford to buy lunch and get a haircut," said International Labor Rights Forum head Judy Gearhart. "Where's the investment in workers today? Are they really just cogs in the wheel?"

Organic cotton farmer Sally Fox.
© 2012 by Paige Green.

THREE

DIRTY LAUNDRY

You are probably wearing jeans as you read this. If you're not, chances are you wore them yesterday. Or you will tomorrow. At any given moment, half the world's population is sporting jeans. Six billion pairs are produced annually. The average American owns seven—one for each day of the week. Beyond basics like underwear and socks, blue jeans are the most popular garment ever.

Blue jeans are made of cotton, one of our oldest crops. Scientists believe cotton has been farmed since 3500 BC. The ancient Greek historian Herodotus described cotton as "a wool exceeding in beauty and goodness that of sheep." When Alexander the Great invaded India with his army in 327–326 BC, he had his troops use cotton for their bedding and saddle pads. Caesar pitched a cotton tent across the Forum in Rome.

About sixty billion pounds of cotton are grown each year across more than one hundred countries. India is the largest producer. China is a close second. And the United States is third. You can find cotton in fishing nets, coffee filters, bandages, disposable diapers—even banknotes: America's paper currency is 75 percent cotton and 25 percent linen. Cotton's most common use, however, is for clothing: 60 percent of all women's apparel contains it. For men, it's 75 percent. For blue jeans, it's 100 percent.

Only 1 percent of all cotton today is organic—meaning it is grown without chemical fertilizers, or pesticides and insecticides, which are chemicals sprayed on plants to kill bugs and disease.

The rest—99 percent of cotton grown today—is treated with chemical fertilizers, pesticides, and insecticides. The World Health Organization (WHO) says that eight out of ten of the most popular cotton pesticides used by farmers in the United States are "hazardous."

Farmers use these dangerous pesticides and herbicides because, in the short term, it costs less to grow cotton with chemicals. Immediate profit is conventional cotton farmers' primary goal.

There are a lot of tales about the birth of denim and jeans. Some historians think denim came from the southern French town of Nîmes—or de Nîmes, [duh-NEEM] as the French say. Some say the explorer Christopher Columbus of the Italian port city of Genoa—or Gênes, in French—used the fabric for his ships' sails and that Genovese sailors wore blue cotton pants.

Fashion scholars now believe that textile mills in Manchester, New Hampshire, invented denim in the nineteenth century, and named it "jean." The mills dyed the denim dark blue with natural indigo that was farmed in the American South. Indigo is one of humanity's oldest natural dyes, extracted from the leaves of the *Indigofera* plant. Indigo was first farmed in America by enslaved people on South Carolina plantations in the mid-eighteenth century, before the American Revolution. It soon became one of the British colony's most successful crops.

In the early 1870s, a tailor in Reno, Nevada, named Jacob Davis wrote to his fabric supplier, Levi Strauss, in San Francisco, and asked for help to mass-produce his most recent design: sturdy denim work pants held together with metal rivets. The pants were such a hit among miners, farmers, and laborers that Davis said, "I cannot make them fast enough."

Davis had an idea: If Strauss would pay the costly fee of $68 to file for a patent, the two men could be business partners, and manufacture the riveted denim trousers in San Francisco. Davis included with his letter an example of the pants. Strauss liked them, and applied for the patent. On May 20, 1873, the patent was granted. Levi Strauss & Co. was founded. It is one of the most successful apparel brands, ever.

The world's oldest surviving Levis can be found in the Vault, the company's archives at its headquarters in San

Francisco. The Vault is watched over by company historian Tracey Panek, a kind, middle-aged woman who reminded me of an elementary school librarian.

On a sunny fall Friday in 2017, Panek welcomed me into the Vault to see the best of Levi's historic collection. We started with a pair from 1879. Panek put on white cotton gloves, pulled open a drawer of the fireproof safe, carefully lifted the pants out, and placed them on a long table.

One-hundred-and-forty-year-old jeans!

They were short, wide, and very faded, with century-old dirt so ground into the thighs, it looked like it would never, ever come out in the wash. Panek explained that, because jeans were expensive, miners would repair and share them until they were completely worn out. "I call them the first sustainable garment, because you could patch them up and pass them on," she said.

The profits from his company made Strauss one of the richest men in California. When he died in 1902, at seventy-three, he left much of his $1.667 million estate to local charities. His four nephews inherited the company. (Strauss never married or had children.)

One of the nephews, Sigmund Stern, and Stern's son-in-law Walter Haas, took charge of the company. They modernized the jeans' design, replacing the button fly with zippers, the suspender buttons with belt loops. And while they continued to buy their denim from Amoskeag

Mills in New Hampshire, they also bought from a new source: the Cone brothers' White Oak Cotton Mills, in Greensboro, North Carolina.

Cone Mills was founded in the mid-1890s by Moses and Ceasar [sic] Cone, two brothers who, like Strauss, were German immigrants. In 1905, they opened a second facility, White Oak Cotton Mills, named for a majestic two-hundred-year-old oak tree that stood nearby.

Much of the denim produced there was dyed with synthetic, or human-made, indigo, developed by the German chemist Adolf von Baeyer in a laboratory and commercialized by the German chemical company BASF in 1897. There were many good reasons for businessmen like the Cone brothers to choose to use synthetic indigo over natural indigo.

Natural indigo comes from the indigo plant, which is grown in fields. At any time during the season, the crop could be ruined by disease, storms, or frost. Synthetic was made in a laboratory, so no threat of destruction.

And natural indigo had a season: It could only be grown from late spring through autumn, which meant there were several months when it wasn't available. Synthetic indigo, which is made of chemicals, could be available anytime.

Synthetic indigo isn't as perfect as everyone thought it was 100 years ago. It is made of several chemicals that we now know are harmful to the environment. But back then, no one knew that. Synthetic indigo seemed to be the best choice, because it was more consistent, and cheaper, than natural indigo. This meant mills like Cone White Oak could weave and dye denim twelve months a year. And weaving twelve months a year meant more profit. By 1914, the natural indigo business had been wiped out. White Oak eventually became the largest denim producer in the world, and Moses was known as the Denim King.

In 1915, the Levi Strauss nephews met with the Cones to discuss Levi's buying denim from White Oak. They closed the deal with what is known as "the Golden Handshake." From then on, Cone exclusively supplied Levi Strauss with denim for its 501 jeans. And blue jeans' popularity steadily grew.

Until the 1980s, most jeans sold had been made of stiff, shrink-to-fit—or "unsanforized"—denim. You would buy unsanforized jeans a size or two larger that you needed, then, to get them to fit, either wash them or—ideally—put them on and sit in a bathtub full of water. Really.

To soften them, you simply had to wear them. A lot. It took a good six months to properly break in a pair of jeans. After a couple of years—*years*—the hems and pocket edges might start to fray, or a knee would split open. The fabric faded to a powdery blue with some whiskering—the sunburst-like streaks that radiate from the fly. It took time and dedication to get your jeans to peak fabulousness.

That is, until the popularization of stonewashing in the 1980s. To stone-wash jeans, unsanforized jeans were thrown into industrial washing machines with volcanic rocks called pumice and tumbled until the denim was faded and broken in. Sometimes jeans would be washed with acid, or workers would scrape the denim with sandpaper and rasps to give the jeans a well-worn look. The whole process—stone washing, sanding, etc.—is called "finishing," and is done in "washhouses"—huge factories that process thousands of jeans a day. Some washhouses—especially those in Los Angeles, America's jeans finishing center—are highly technical and follow strict worker safety and environmental norms. But a lot do not, as I saw in Ho Chi Minh City on a steamy April morning in 2018.

Vietnam's textile and apparel industry has existed since about the 1950s, and for about fifty years, it remained quite small. When I visited the country in early 1993 and drove from Hanoi south to Da Nang, I saw a few clothing factories. But it was clear, with the emerald lawn of rice paddies across much of the land, that the nation's economy was largely based on agriculture.

Trade agreements and globalization changed that landscape. By 2018, there were roughly 6,000 textile and garment production companies in Vietnam, employing 2.5 million workers, and accounting for about 16 percent of the country's exports and more than $30 billion in revenue.

Much of the work is jeans finishing, and I saw that firsthand.

On the industrial outskirts of Ho Chi Minh, a local denim expert and I drove up to a run-down, warehouse-like factory behind a big gate. Inside, there were about two hundred young Vietnamese, washing and distressing jeans.

The fluorescent lighting was poor, and the temperature was *so* hot—100 degrees Fahrenheit, easy. There was no air-conditioning; only giant fans, which didn't do much to cool the place.

Brand-new, midnight-blue jeans were piled high on metal tables. Young men in butter-yellow T-shirts, trousers—usually jeans—and knee-high rubber boots took the jeans and stuffed them into monster-sized washing machines. Other young, booted men pulled sopping wet jeans out of other machines. An inch of navy-blue water stood on the floor. The men did not wear gloves, and their hands were stained black. Some of the machines were older types that require twenty liters, or five gallons, of water to wash one kilogram—about two pounds, or three pairs—of jeans. Others were less piggy, using only five liters—or a bit more than one gallon—of water per kilo of jeans. Manufacturers "know how wasteful this is," my guide told me. But they don't care. "Their business is about washing, not about worrying about the planet," he explained.

The wet jeans were thrown into massive dryers. Some of the jeans were treated with chemicals and baked in a giant oven to replicate fade patterns like whiskering. In another huge room, young men and women in sky-blue T-shirts—each department had its designated color—were sanding jean knees and thighs by hand, like a carpenter works on wood. This work is called "distressing," and the people who do it are known as "distressers." Some of them wore medical masks to prevent inhalation of denim dust, but most did not.

Each pair of jeans went from new to wrecked in under a minute. The workers' focus was intense—they didn't speak or notice anything happening around them. At the time I visited, the sanders each processed at least four hundred pairs of jeans a day, six days a week, not including overtime.

And that was the hand distressers. The machine

distressers worked even faster. I watched one woman tackle cutoff shorts with what looked like an oversized dental drill that was so loud and high-pitched, it hurt my ears. She ground the front and back pockets and hems of those shorts to a fashionably holey state in ten seconds. Six pairs a minute. All day long. She was unmasked, which meant she was inhaling the dangerous denim fibers she sanded off those shorts, in a room where it was hard not to sneeze because of the dust.

This all apparently compared well to the washhouses of Xintang, the town in China that claims to be the "jeans capital of the world." Each year, 200,000 garment workers in Xintang's 3,000 factories and workshops produce 300 million pairs of jeans—800,000 pairs a day. The local water treatment plant closed years ago, leaving factories to dump dye waste directly into the East River. The river turned black, and the plants and fish died. Xintang's streets are dusted blue. And many garment workers have reportedly suffered from skin rashes and lung infections from breathing in the denim dust.

It didn't have to be this way, as cotton expert Sally Fox explained to me. We were sitting at a simple wooden table in Fox's mobile home on her 130-acre farm northwest of Sacramento, California, on an early autumn morning.

The living room was lined with rows of oak filing cabinets full of files on cotton: studies, orders, swatches. The windows were open. The quiet was broken only by her merino sheep bleating in the pasture, a rooster crowing in the barnyard, and the north wind rippling through the shade tree out front.

Five foot seven, with short, snow-white hair and an honest smile, Fox was dressed in a water-blue denim shirt and caramel denim jeans. I had come to see her because she is considered by many in the industry to be the mother of modern organic cotton. A native Northern Californian, Fox bought her first spindle at twelve with her babysitting money and started spinning wool, cotton—anything she could find. While in the Peace Corps in Gambia in 1979 and 1980, she helped develop natural ways to fight pests. For the last forty years or so, she has been breeding and farming colored organic cotton in Arizona and California.

Colored cotton is just that: Instead of having plants that produce the traditional white boll, as the cotton tuft is called, Fox grows varieties that produce bolls that are naturally tinted blue, green, or brown. Colored cotton has existed as long as white cotton. Back in the eighteenth century, the Chinese grew a pale-yellow variety used to make a type of cloth called "nankeen" that was popular in the American colonies. "Everyone wanted nankeen gold trousers," she said.

After Fox finished her university studies, she worked for a plant breeder in California. While cleaning the greenhouse one day, she opened a drawer and found a bag of brown cotton. She was charmed by it and thought, If it can be spun, people will want it, because you don't have to dye it. She ordered seeds from the USDA and planted them in pots in the greenhouse.

Fox was so pleased at how well the cotton turned out, she planted a quarter acre of land near Bakersfield, the capital of California cotton farming. "The next year," she said, "I rented an acre, then five, then eleven, and on and on." She discovered that tannins, the organic substance that gave the cotton bolls their color, also made the cotton plants naturally disease and insect resistant. So she farmed organically, back when "no one was doing organic cotton," she said. "No one."

She landed a few production contracts. One was with Levi's. They wanted to use Fox's cotton to make a caramel-colored denim. The jeans Fox was wearing the morning we met were made of that denim. Levi's and Fox negotiated a three-year deal. She would supply colored cotton seeds to farmers in West Texas, who would grow the cotton, spin it, and weave it into denim. Then Levi's would buy the finished denim and turn it into clothing.

The first year, the farmers planted one hundred acres' worth of Fox's seed, and Levi's bought the denim. The second year, the order was upped to a thousand acres. And the third year, it was three thousand acres. "The farmers made so much money," Fox remembered. "They were really happy."

As was Levi's. The jeans and jackets were "wildly popular," she said. "This could change the world," Levi's head Bob Haas told her. "If you could get a hundred thousand acres' worth of seed, I can do it, I can make it happen."

This time, Fox and Haas didn't draw up a contract. "I just made it my goal because I wanted so much to be part of the reduction of this enormous environmental disaster," she told me. "I got all the seed, and I paid a million dollars."

In 1996, Levi's reported a record-breaking $7.1 billion a year in sales—more than Nike. But a series of complicated business decisions put the company in financial difficulty, and sales fell unexpectedly. Levi's canceled its colored cotton order with Sally Fox.

She went bankrupt.

Once again, a fashion company's obsession with profit—its greed—led it to make business decisions without regard for the lives of the people it worked with.

"I lost everything," Fox told me sadly.

The abrupt cancellation also meant that Levi's wasn't going to be making environmentally friendly, dye-free jeans after all. Quite the contrary: It would continue to pollute on a massive scale.

The company had, in essence, scrapped Levi Strauss's

original mission one hundred and fifty years earlier—to commercially produce the world's first and most sustainable clothing item—*and* destroyed the life and business of Sally Fox. All to rake in *more* money.

It was a dark turn for what had long been an admirable, honorable company. And it echoed what was happening throughout the fashion industry at that moment: the sacrificing of integrity, humanity, and the planet, all for the sake of profit.

For much of the twentieth century, Levi's was known in the apparel industry as a company with a conscience. In part, that was because the family that ran it—Strauss's descendants, the Haases—were devout Jews who carried on his commitment to charity, and in part because the company was headquartered in politically liberal San Francisco. In the 1970s, Levi's chief executive Walter Haas Jr. brought in a religious ethicist to advise him on how to have more responsible business practices. When Walter Jr.'s son, Bob—a former Peace Corps volunteer in the Ivory Coast—took the helm in 1984, he carried on that belief. "A company's values—what it stands for, what its people believe in—are crucial to its competitive success," he said.

But by the late 1990s—when Bob Haas Jr. told Sally Fox to personally fund and plant a million dollars' worth of colored cotton, then canceled the order—Levi's was in financial trouble. To get the company back on its feet, it hired Philip Marineau, former president and chief executive of Pepsi-Cola North America, as chief executive. He was the first non–Strauss family member to run Levi's. His reorganization plan was simple: Close Levi's-owned factories everywhere, and subcontract *all* production.

One of those factories was in Blue Ridge, Georgia. It had been in operation for forty-three years. Levi's had been generous with the town. It donated to the hospital, schools, nursing homes, the public library, and Little League teams. It helped pay for a Jaws of Life rescue tool for car crashes and the field lights at the local stadium. "They've just allowed us to have a lot of things we couldn't have had," the high school principal, Doug Davenport, said.

That was over. Hundreds of people lost their jobs making belt loops and sewing zippers into jeans. Local kids stopped taking swimming lessons at the county rec center, because their parents, who used to work at the factory, could no longer afford to pay the $20 enrollment fee. Many families moved away in search of work, which meant there were fewer students, so the school board fired teachers. "Money is going to be tight," said Fannin County's recreation director, Bernie Hodgkins. "It's going to devastate this little county."

In all, Marineau fired 25,000 Levi's employees in six

years. In 2004, he reportedly earned $6.3 million and was up for an additional $4 million bonus over the next two years. At the close of those two years—at the age of sixty—he stepped down. In his retirement, he would be paid $1.2 million by Levi's each year, for life.

After her bankruptcy, Sally Fox regrouped. She traded her farm in Kern County for the one where we were sitting on that October morning. She arrived with a truck, a trailer, and her seeds. She kept breeding and growing small amounts of colored and organic cotton, to make sure the varieties she had nurtured would still be available when farmers wanted to buy them.

Levi's business choices were so hurtful to its workers, I decided to pay a visit to David Weil, dean of the Heller School for Social Policy and Management at Brandeis University, and ask him why companies behaved this way.

He told me that business's obsession with profits has corrupted the supply chain, from raw materials to labor. That greed has given us offshoring, layoffs, poorly paid and treated workers, shoddy factories, tragedies.

"What's viewed as acceptable behavior has deteriorated," he said. Some fashion businesses, like Levi's, used to have shared values that were honorable and guided how the companies behaved. But those values disappeared during the 1990s and early 2000s—the period when the industry went global, and fast.

To change this behavior, Weil believes state and federal agencies must step in and bring "the tops of these companies to the table." Companies need to be forced—perhaps by law or regulation, like back in Frances Perkins's day—to rethink what they demand of factories, and workers, and at what price. Ultimately, Weil said, brands will have to accept the idea of smaller profits.

It also means "consumers will have to pay somewhat more" for clothes, he said. "If consumers want eleven-dollar garments that they are going to feel good about, wake up."

In short, the industry needs a massive reset.

Today, fashion executives "dictate everything they want in their supply chain to an incredible degree," Weil said. "They will send back an order when the dyes aren't right—they monitor that precisely.

"But," he continued, "somehow, it's unreasonable to make sure that there is adherence to fire emergency escapes rules, and you aren't operating in a building like Rana Plaza. Either you start attacking that piece of this problem, through a combination of consumer and NGO pressure, and cooperation of governments."

Or, he said, you come up with "a different production model, entirely."

PART TWO

Designer Natalie Chanin picking cotton on the Lentz farm in Trinity, Alabama.
© 2012 by Rinne Allen.

FOUR

FIELD TO FORM

Natalie Chanin is a fashion designer based in Florence, Alabama. For much of the twentieth century, Florence was the Cotton T-shirt Capital of the World. In the T-shirt factories of Florence, "they used cotton that was grown around here," Chanin told me.

We were having lunch together at the headquarters of her company, Alabama Chanin, which is located in a former T-shirt factory in Florence.

"There was actually a knitting machine in this building, and the dye house was back behind us," she said. "This"—sweeping her hand around the wide-open space where we were sitting—"was a sewing floor. Just rows and rows of machinery. Hundreds and hundreds of hemmers. Ralph [Lauren], Tommy [Hilfiger], and Walt Disney all produced here."

When NAFTA—or the North American Free Trade Agreement—went into effect in the early 1990s, fashion companies began to move clothing production from towns like Florence, Alabama, to Mexico, and later to other countries with cheaper labor, such as Honduras, China, and Bangladesh. NAFTA ended Florence's reign as the T-shirt Capital of the World. Factories closed, and workers went on unemployment.

"In 1993, five thousand people worked in this two-block radius," Chanin said. "And that didn't include all the service industries—restaurants, day-care centers, gas stations. There used to be twenty dye houses in this town." All those businesses closed, and the town became very poor. "When manufacturing collapsed here, every-thing collapsed."

Now, twenty-five years on, Chanin and her friend Louisiana-born fashion designer Billy Reid are trying to bring some of those jobs back to Florence.

At her headquarters, called The Factory, Natalie Chanin and her team of thirty run the women's clothing brand Alabama Chanin. They specialize in flowing organic-cotton dresses and smart tailoring, and everything they sell is produced in and around Florence.

On Florence's main street, Billy Reid has his offices and a shop—one of twelve stores in the United States when I visited in 2018. He specializes in American-style cloth-ing, such as linen suits, denim work shirts, cotton dresses, and high-quality jeans.

To staff their companies, Chanin and Reid have hired

young talents from big cities, which has given Florence a real burst of energy. There are now all sorts of trendy new restaurants and hotels, a microbrewery, and a record company cofounded by local Grammy-winning musician John Paul White. Thanks to Chanin and Reid, Florence has come back to life.

What Chanin and Reid are doing is known as "slow fashion": a movement of makers, designers, and manufacturers around the world who, in response to fast-fashion and globalization, have slowed everything down. They don't want to be the biggest brand in the world, or to make the most money. They want to have a good life, in a nice town, and create beautiful products that people will appreciate and keep for a long time. It's about treating workers well, Chanin said, and "buying from the person down the street whose face you know and love."

Chanin believes education is key. At The Factory, she has a school to teach sewing, and has made a short documentary film called *Stitch,* about the art of Southern quilting. Sewing, she said, "is a skill that is dying out in this country." She believes we should "be able to make our clothes." If we lose the knowledge of sewing, she asks, "What happens to the culture?"

Chanin grew up around cotton fields. Both of her grandfathers were farmers. Her grandmothers sewed at home.

One "made everybody's underwear, nightgowns, every-thing," she said. Her grandmothers showed her how to sew too. She studied fashion and textile design at North Carolina State University in the 1980s, then moved to New York City, where she worked as a design assistant for a teenage clothing brand. What she encountered there made her rethink her career dreams.

"I spent a lot of time overseas, and I saw a lot of things that I don't think are right—things that you don't want human beings to do," she told me. She heard horror stories too. One friend, who worked for the fast-fashion brand Gap, "told me she visited a dye house in India and the dye was just pouring directly into a river," Chanin said. "And ten feet down the river, kids were getting water and drink-ing it. They were drinking blue dye. The river was blue. I thought: If that's how I have to make fashion, then I don't want to make fashion."

In 1990, Chanin moved to Vienna, Austria, and worked for MTV. She returned to New York in 2000, for what was supposed to be a short break. She spent her days at Goodwill stores, buying T-shirts. She'd cut them up, sew them back together, and decorate them with unusual embroideries that showed the knots and dangling threads. "That defined our style," she said.

She wanted to launch a proper company, but she needed help—sewing help, production help. She went to work-shops in New York's Garment District and asked if they could copy her embroidery work. "Nobody could understand what I was talking about," she said. "Then I realized it looked like a quilting stitch, and if I wanted to get it made as I wanted, I needed to come home to Alabama, where people still quilted."

She moved into a house her aunt owned, set up a few sewing machines and a desk, and found quilters around Florence to do her embroideries. This was the beginning of her first company, called Project Alabama. She sold the clothes at trendy fashion stores in New York, Los Angeles, and London. The T-shirts were expensive—up to $400 apiece. But they sold well. She added dresses and suits to the collection. All were made of organic cotton or recycled materials, and sewed by seamstresses in Florence.

I first met Chanin about this time, at a hotel in Los Angeles. She was in town to check out LA Fashion Week—a week of fashion shows and parties that celebrate brands from the region. I was invited to Chanin's hotel room by a mutual friend, and I brought along my then four-year-old daughter. Chanin sat on the sofa, with a piece of cotton jersey—like T-shirt fabric—in her lap. She held a threaded needle in her right hand, and the fingers of her left were running down the strands, as if she were massaging them. "This is called 'loving the thread,'" she explained to my daughter. She said it was a Southern practice to prepare the thread for sewing.

During the spinning process, the thread's fibers are

twisted until they are super tight. "When you sew and your thread tangles, it's because it has too much tension," she said. "One of the traditions I was taught is 'loving your thread': As you pull it through your fingers, the oils in your skin coat the strands, and you release the tension. Then it doesn't tangle as much." She demonstrated this to my daughter, and the two of them sat there, calmly drawing thread through their fingertips.

Chanin's sales were good. "But as we all know, building a fashion business is hard," she told me. "And building a fashion business based on artisan handwork in the US is extremely difficult." Finally, in 2006, she closed the company in New York, and started again, with everything based in Florence, Alabama, where the rent, the cost of living—everything, really—was much more affordable. She called the new company Alabama Chanin.

Her timing was perfect. Thanks to the internet, working from home had become easy. And with smartphone and tablet apps, small businesses could set up selling online. Until those inventions came around, starting a global company in a small town seemed impossible. Places like Florence were too far away—too disconnected—from major business capitals like New York, London, and Paris. But the technology that helped fast-fashion giants Zara and H&M go global also made it possible for slow fashion companies such as Alabama Chanin to exist and succeed in small towns like Florence.

- - -

Chanin rented space in a former T-shirt factory, and moved her company in. Her studio, walled off by plywood and corrugated metal partitions, has worktables and a dozen sewing machines. She buys her fabrics from Signet Mills in Spartanburg, South Carolina. Her preferred fabric is T-shirt–like cloth, called "jersey," made of organic Texas cotton. And she works with a small, local dye company for her indigo pieces. Rather than print on her fabrics like Mary Katrantzou does, Chanin uses stencils—graphic shapes cut out of cardboard or sheets of plastic. She spray paints the patterns on the cloth with an airbrush gun.

Once the fabric is cut and stenciled, and the embroidery materials are chosen, the team puts everything in a bag called a "kit." When a customer places an order online, one of Chanin's freelance seamstresses is assigned the job. The seamstress drives to the Alabama Chanin headquarters, picks up the kit, sews the garment in a day or two, numbers and signs it, and brings it back to the studio to be packaged and sent to the customer.

"There are a lot of people who ask, 'How do you know it's not child labor?'" Chanin told me. "And I say, 'Well, we've known Miss Betty now for sixteen years. She's eighty-six years old. She only does one particular kind of work. She doesn't have any kids at her house crocheting snap covers.' And it's why we have a rule that our sewers have to all live within an hour and a half of us; you have to pick up and drop off your work yourself. If somebody's coming in and taking fifty kits a week, it's a pretty good sign that they're not doing it themselves. It's just a more personal relationship. And it's all women."

"It's all women?" I asked.

"It's all women," she said.

There were plenty of people along the way who told Chanin that producing high fashion in an honest and safe way in America—paying and treating her workers well—was impossible. "But we've stuck to our standards, even when it wasn't the easiest thing to do," she said. "And we've made it."

Sure, there are times when doing everything in northwest Alabama has been difficult, and sometimes Chanin has felt disconnected from the happening fashion centers of New York and Los Angeles.

But there are great advantages to being "hyperlocal," as she calls it.

"I'm 100 percent self-owned—no partners," she said. "We invest in young people and train them well. We have a deep commitment to our community. I have been able to raise my children and live a creative life that makes me happy and do good and important works. I like where I've landed and what we have created. And I'm proud of having been active in bringing something back to my hometown and contributing to its future."

- - -

Like Chanin, Billy Reid had to stumble to realize that small-town slow fashion was the way to go. Born in 1964 and raised in Amite City, Louisiana, Reid is a second-generation fashion retailer; his mother, T. J. Reid, had a dress boutique in his grandmother's former home. "My mother didn't care if customers shopped," Reid told me during my visit to Florence. "They might just come to talk and gossip."

Reid had bigger plans. In 1998, he founded William Reid, a Dallas-based fashion brand, with his friends Katy and K. P. McNeill. In 2000, they moved the company to New York. All was going well until September, 2001: The day after his fashion show, terrorists attacked New York City, destroying the Twin Towers of the World Trade Center and killing more than 2,500 people. The economic recession immediately caused by the September 11 attacks was too much. Reid closed his company. "We lost everything," he told me.

He and his wife, Jeanne, moved to her hometown of Florence with their two small children and two big dogs. Katy and K. P. McNeill had an idea: Create a lifestyle brand that celebrated Reid's Southern roots. They wrote up a business plan and presented it to him. He liked it. The McNeills moved to Florence too, and in 2004, the trio launched a new fashion brand there, called Billy Reid.

The company has done very well, and now has more than a dozen stores around America. "Being in Florence differentiated us right off the bat," K.P. told me in 2016, at the company's offices above Reid's shop. "If Billy were just another designer in New York, it'd be so much tougher. I don't think we'd be able to make money if we were there."

In 2011, K. P. McNeill was driving past some local cotton fields during harvest when he had an idea: Why not grow cotton in Florence and turn it into clothes in Alabama?

McNeill explained his idea to Reid and Chan, and they loved it.

Back before NAFTA, Chanin said, the local textile and apparel businesses "were growing the cotton; they were ginning the cotton; they were processing it." The cotton went "straight from field to form"—from the cotton plant all the way to clothing. Reid and Chanin wanted to return to that way of making clothes, but with a twist: It would be organic. Today, only 1 percent of cotton is organically grown—meaning cotton farmed without chemical fertilizers, pesticides, or herbicides. The rest of the world's cotton is farmed with chemicals. Chanin and Reid wanted to prove they could still grow cotton as it had been for thousands of years before industrialization—without chemicals and machinery.

"So many people were betting against us and saying, 'You can't grow cotton unless you use pesticides. The bugs will eat it. It will be gone. Good luck, ha ha,'" said Alabama farmer Lisa Lentz, who, with her husband, Jimmy Lentz, owned the land where Chanin, Reid, and McNeill grew the cotton.

"We didn't water. We didn't do anything," Chanin said. "Weeds started coming up, and we weeded by hand, but in some sections the weeds just kind of took over. And the cotton still grew and thrived."

For the harvest, in the spring of 2012, "people drove from all over," Chanin said. Chanin and Reid asked friends and friends of friends to help them harvest the cotton, and they did the work alongside these volunteers. "Some folks flew in from San Francisco. And we had a party. Six acres. Six hundred pounds. Three hundred people."

The cotton was bagged and sent to a local factory and run through a cotton gin to remove the seeds. Then it was shipped to Hill Spinning Mill, a fifty-year-old mill in North Carolina, to be spun into thread. The mill's machines were cleaned before the organic cotton was processed, so the chemicals from traditional cotton wouldn't contaminate it. The mill owner said he had never seen such clean cotton—the result of handpicking. Most cotton today is picked by machine.

Some of the thread was sent to Gina Locklear of

the Little River Sock Mill in Fort Payne, Alabama, to make socks. Locklear—known as the Sock Queen of Alabama—is a second-generation mill owner. Her parents, Terry and Regina, opened the plant—named Emi-G, for Gina and her sister, Emily—in 1991 and made white sport socks for Russell Athletic.

Back then, Fort Payne was called the Sock Capital of the World. Its more than 150 factories produced one out of every eight pairs worldwide. Then the Central America Free Trade Agreement (CAFTA)—a trade deal similar to NAFTA, but with Central America—went into effect and Fort Payne lost its business to factories in Honduras. The Locklears had almost no orders, but they knew if they closed their factory, they'd never reopen. "We'd just come here and sit," Terry Locklear said.

In 2008, at the age of twenty-eight, Gina stepped up. A sincere environmentalist, she wanted to combine her passions for sustainability and socks. At the family mill, she produced a line of organic cotton socks she called Zkano (pronounced "zuh-kah-NO"), based on an Alabama Native American word that "loosely translates as 'a state of being good,'" she told me. The colors are bold, with jazzy graphic designs. In 2013, Locklear introduced a second line, Little River Sock Mill, a collection in softer tones and patterns. All sold well; the factory was humming again.

Locklear had already collaborated with Chanin and Reid on a few projects. So when Chanin reached out for this one, "Oh, I was excited!" Locklear told me. "I have admired Natalie and Billy for a long time—before I started making socks—because of the positive light they were shining on our communities and our state. And now they were growing cotton in our state too. That was wonderful."

The couple of hundred pairs of socks Locklear produced were natural—no patterns, no dyeing. "Our technicians were really impressed—they said it ran really well through the machines," she recalled. "I remember them saying: 'Great cotton.'"

The rest of the Chanin-Reid cotton was woven by Green Textile (now Signet Mills) in Spartanburg, South Carolina, into cloth—about seven hundred yards' worth—and sent back to Florence, where it was made into T-shirts.

Chanin gave me one of the V-neck T-shirts. Made of a soft, dense vanilla jersey that is solidly seamed, it is one of the best-made, most comfortable shirts I have ever owned.

Tower Mill in Stalybridge, England.
© 2016 by Chris Bull/Alamy Stock Photo.

FIVE

RIGHTSHORING

Chanin and Reid showed me that slow fashion on a small to medium scale was possible, profitable, and sensible. But could their thoughtful local approach to business be expanded from small workshops to larger factories, where there are hundreds, or thousands, of workers? Could what Chanin and Reid were doing—slow fashion—be a way to return manufacturing to countries like the United States, Great Britain, and France, all these years after government trade agreements encouraged companies to move the jobs offshore?

That's what I was about to find out in Cottonopolis, of all places.

On a mouse-gray November morning, I traveled east of Manchester, England, to Stalybridge, an old mill town that, in 1845, the German writer Friedrich Engels described as "repulsive," consumed by "shocking filth."

Today, most of Stalybridge's old mills have been turned into apartment buildings, offices, supermarkets, even gyms. Stalybridge has become a nice middle-class suburb.

It has also become a center for cotton milling again. Tower Mill, an enormous redbrick factory with a tall smokestack, is the headquarters for a new company called English Fine Cottons. And it is spinning cotton again for the first time since the 1950s.

I happened to visit on English Fine Cottons's second full day of operation and witnessed the first large-scale cotton spinning production in the United Kingdom in more than thirty years.

The company's commercial director Tracy Hawkins welcomed me. A hearty blonde in her early fifties with a lot of experience in the British apparel industry, she confessed she was extremely tired. In six months, "we built a modern mill from scratch," she said. "But it's done, and it's working."

English Fine Cottons was founded by two Manchester-born-and-raised businessmen, Brendan McCormack and Steve Shaughnessy. For several years, they have owned the historic Tame Valley Mill, where they spin the yarn for Kevlar, a sturdy technical fabric used for everything from racing sails to bulletproof vests. (While Britain's apparel industry's textile business had long ago moved offshore, closing factories throughout the country, industrial tech fabrics like Kevlar remained in demand, and were produced in the country.)

Over the years, McCormack and Shaughnessy received requests to process cotton, but they said no, since it wasn't their business. Then, in 2014, Tower Mill, which sits directly across the street from Tame Valley Mill, came up for sale.

Tower Mill was built in 1885, and at its peak, it had forty-four thousand spindles, spinning cotton. Since closing in 1955, Tower Mill has housed several different sorts of businesses. In the early 2000s, there was a plan to turn it into a luxury apartment building, like so many other old mills in the region. McCormack and Shaughnessy decided to take it over, and reopen it as a cotton mill. They wanted to make it "a place of excellence," Hawkins said, "producing well-crafted yarns."

With the help of government loans and grants, McCormack and Shaughnessy bought Tower Mill, restored it, and refitted it with the best and smartest computer-run machines available. They decided they would only spin the world's finest cotton. They hired a Yorkshireman, who specialized in running high-tech cotton mills in South Africa, to be in charge of production.

In the pre-tech days, owners relied on Manchester's damp weather to keep down the "fly," as filaments floating in the air like snow are called. Today, the cotton travels through a circuit of giant tubes from one machine to the next. There are blowers that separate the fibers; blenders that mix the various grades of cotton; combers that pull out the short filaments; or, my favorite, the "foreign-particle remover," a big glass box that looks like an oversized cinema popcorn-maker stuffed full of cotton. Lasers scan the cotton for seeds, leaves, or twigs, and when a piece of debris is detected, a needle-precise air jet blasts it out.

All is controlled by lab techs at computers in a sterile room above the factory floor. The air in the factory is changed out twenty-five to thirty times an hour. Modern cotton spinning, Hawkins told me, is "all about having clean air."

The cotton is sped through various processors until "it has a fantastic luster, it's light, and it's straight," Hawkins said. At each stop, it was purer, fluffier, prettier—exactly how you dream about cotton. During high-speed spinning, there is still "fly." But instead of relying on the damp air to keep it down, or, as in the nineteenth century, children with little brooms to sweep between the spindles, the machines are equipped with vacuum robots. This is a much safer, and cleaner, system. Better for the environment. And *much* better for the workers.

The cream-colored yarn is sent to Blackburn Yarn Dyers, one of Britain's last traditional dye houses, to be tinted. Hawkins showed me spools of finished product in gray, navy, and off-white. It was thin and smooth, like dental floss. Eventually, a local weaver would turn it into socks for the British retailer Marks & Spencer.

By reopening Tower Mill, McCormack and Shaughnessy created more than 100 jobs. English Fine Cottons produced 100 tons of yarn in its first year of business, and up to 450 tons in 2018. When I last spoke to Hawkins, in the fall of 2018, she said demand was so great, they had to hire more people, and the mill was running 24 hours a day, 7 days a week. At that point, English Fine Cottons was the only major cotton mill in Britain.

Reshoring is the act of bringing back to the United States and Europe the manufacturing that moved offshore after NAFTA and during the globalization boom. Reshoring is happening now, especially for fashion.

And what English Fine Cottons is doing is what I call "rightshoring": reopening factories—often in long-closed, or abandoned buildings—and filling them with the latest machines and technology. It's all very automated. "Robotics and digitization mean we can produce efficiently, locally," said Paul Donovan, global chief economist at the bank UBS Wealth Management. Like at English Fine Cottons, with its air jet cleaning systems and robotic vacuums.

Surprisingly, technology may finally transform textile and apparel manufacturing to something more personal and honorable. Clothes don't have to be made by poorly paid, poorly treated workers using old, dangerous machinery. They can be produced on quiet, clean factory floors, controlled by tech-trained assistants, or by robots run by technicians from sterile rooms. Automation may not create thousands of manufacturing jobs, but the ones it does create—a hundred here, a hundred there, like at English Fine Cottons—will be good, safe, and well-paying. Technology can bring humanity to the supply chain.

Rightshoring has revived North Carolina's and South Carolina's textile and apparel industry, with the opening or renovation of hundreds of factories that are now as high tech as English Fine Cottons's. Some of those factories are owned by Chinese companies. "I never thought the Chinese would be the ones bringing textile jobs back" to America, said Lancaster County Economic Development Corporation president Keith Tunnell. But they have.

NAFTA and globalization didn't only take jobs away from places like Alabama and the Carolinas. The New York Garment District was wounded deeply too. As the clothing manufacturing jobs were transferred offshore to Mexico, Central America, and Asia, factories closed. In New York City's Garment District, like in Stalybridge, those big, empty buildings were transformed into luxury apartments and offices. For the last twenty years, there have been several movements and organizations dedicated to saving the Garment District. Ideas have included moving all Garment District fashion companies to Sunset Park, a neighborhood across the East River in Brooklyn.

The most effective action, however, has been the loyalty of New York–based designers like Maria Cornejo (pronounced "cor-NAY-ho"), who has a women's wear brand called Zero + Maria Cornejo. (The + is said as "plus.") For it, she has almost everything made in New York.

Cornejo was born in Chile, and educated in Great Britain. Back in the late 1980s, she worked in Paris for the UK mass fashion retailer Jigsaw and saw firsthand what she calls "the false economy."

The false economy, she said, is the idea that a company saves money on one side of the business—for example, by offshoring work in a cheaper place in a faraway land—then spends a lot of money shipping everything from that place to its warehouse in the United States or Europe. Another example of the false economy: saving money by contracting production in unsafe factories because those factories are cheap, then spending a lot of money on inspectors to make sure the workers aren't in danger.

At the company where Cornejo worked, her managers would send her to Hong Kong, flying business class, and pay for her to stay at a luxury hotel. Then they'd "nickel-and-dime" the customers she was going to see—meaning they would cut costs at every level of production to save money, especially on how much they wanted to pay the workers. "They'd say, 'Well, we're going to save a dollar on a sweater, but we're going to ship it halfway across the world,'" she explained as we sat in her book-stuffed office in downtown New York. "It didn't make sense to me. It just didn't."

Production was "a crazy system," she said. The company's designers, who were based in Europe and the United States, would email designs and the list of details, such as fabric, zippers, buttons, to a factory in Asia for the first versions of the designs, called "samples," to be made. After many conversations, by email and by phone, the finished samples would be shipped from the factory in Asia to the home office in Europe to be reviewed and, more often than not, rejected. Jigsaw was one of many fashion companies working like this—in fact, most did. One major brand in New York—a household name—would order *six hundred* samples in China, then "cut it down to two hundred," Cornejo said. "Can you imagine the waste?"

"I just wanted to make everything in one place and, even if it was a T-shirt, have control from beginning to end—how it looks, how it was made, who made it," she explained. "I wanted to know those people." She wanted to bring the manufacturing back to the country—even the city—where the rest of the team worked. She wanted to rightshore.

In 1996, she moved from Paris to New York City, and took over an old garage on Mott Street, in downtown Manhattan. Two years later, she opened a store there with a sewing workshop in the back. Her plan was to make and sell "interesting, easy clothes that you could afford to wear," she said. She called the brand Zero because she "wanted it to be just about the product," she said. And not all the hype that often comes with fashion. When she learned there was already a big German fashion company called Zero, she renamed hers Zero + Maria Cornejo.

Her team was tight, and international. Jiang Huang, an immigrant from Shanghai, sewed the samples there in the workshop. Tonya, from Russia, handled knitwear, like sweaters. Lynn, from China, was in charge of silks. "And I cut everything," Cornejo said. The labels read: *Made at 225 Mott Street*. And she sold the clothes in her shop out front. "I remember one day a lady arguing with me about the price of my clothes, and I said, 'You see all those people working in the back? They live in New York. They get paid fair wages. We pay this rent. It's not like the clothes that have been made by child labor,'" in a poor country on the other side of the world.

Cornejo only sells women's wear and a few accessories, such as belts and shoes. "I've never been interested in having a pair of underpants with my name on them," she said, referring to megafashion brands like Calvin Klein, who *do* have underwear with the company name on the elastic waistband. "It doesn't appeal to me, that whole thing of more, more, more, more, more for the sake of it . . . Growth isn't necessarily getting bigger, and bigger, and bigger. No, it's doing things in the right way, and creating the right environment. Fine-tuning."

By 2008, Cornejo's shop-atelier had blossomed into a full-fledged company and it was time to move. She found a perfect spot on Bleecker Street in Greenwich Village: a one-hundred-year-old building where she could have her shop on the ground floor, studios and office on the first and second floors, and storage in the basement.

When I visited, the second-floor workroom was filled with metal rolling racks with hangers holding fabric, paper patterns, and clothes. Across the hall, Mr. Huang and his design team were conducting fittings for the spring-summer collection.

Cornejo has almost all her ready-to-wear produced in New York City, making her one of about fifty brands to manufacture at least three-quarters of their output there. Most of her suppliers are based in the Garment District. "Thirty-sixth Street, Thirty-eighth Street," she said. "When there is any drama at the factory, my people jump on the subway and go right up and check on it."

Since 2009, Cornejo has produced four collections a year—two for the runway during New York Fashion Week, two for showroom appointments only. She has twenty-eight employees, and does about $10 million a year in sales—the size Natalie Chanin is shooting for. It's a tiny amount compared to the $5 to $10 *billion* that the megabrands such as Dior, Gucci, Chanel, and Louis Vuitton sell every year. But it's a respectable size for a one-woman company.

Sarah Bellos in her indigo fields.

SIX

MY BLUE HEAVEN

Indigo is the dye that makes jeans blue. Natural indigo has existed for thousands of years—the Egyptians used it at the time of the pyramids. Synthetic indigo, invented by the German chemical company BASF in 1897, is made up of chemicals, many of which are poisonous to the environment and to humans. But because it is easier to make and use, synthetic indigo is what almost *all* jeans companies use today. Natural indigo entrepreneur Sarah Bellos, the founder of Stony Creek Colors, wants to change that. She wants natural indigo–dyed jeans to be available to everyone.

On a summer morning, I drove to Goodlettsville, Tennessee, a country town about fifteen miles north of Nashville, to see Sarah Bellos and learn about natural indigo. When I walked up to her office, I noticed muddy boots lined up outside the front door. "We were out in the fields this morning," she told me as she welcomed me. Thirty-three and fresh-faced, she was dressed in a gray T-shirt and jeans made of denim dyed with her indigo. Its cornflower blue was as vivid as a sapphire. Her fingernails were black from indigo dye.

"The fields" were thirty-five acres in nearby Greenbrier, Tennessee, where she has hired ten farmers to plant and grow indigo. She regularly checks on progress, and helps with the harvest. At her lab, she converts the leaves into dye, which she sells to jeans manufacturers.

Indigo has not been farmed commercially in the United States for more than a hundred years. About ten years after German chemical company BASF invented synthetic indigo, most denim producers switched from natural indigo to synthetic indigo to dye their cloth, and the natural indigo industry collapsed. Denim companies prefer synthetic indigo because it is reliable—it's always the same color, and it's always available. Natural indigo is seasonal—it is planted in the spring, harvested in the fall. At any time during the growing season, the fields could be destroyed by storms or disease.

Today, almost all the denim we wear—99.99 percent— is dyed with synthetic indigo. The reason? Because synthetic indigo is easier and cheaper to produce and use than natural indigo.

But synthetic indigo is linked to serious environmental and health issues. Synthetic indigo is "made of ten chemicals—including petroleum, benzene, cyanide, formaldehyde—that are toxic or harmful to humans," Bellos told me.

Sometimes, wastewater from jeans factories is dumped directly into rivers. The rivers turn black, which blocks the sunlight. Without sunlight, the plants and fish die. The chemicals kill plants and fish too. I saw one of these polluted rivers next to a former jeans factory in Vietnam. The water was thick and black, like tar. It smelled *awful*. The river was dead.

The denim industry uses synthetic indigo for the same reason fashion companies have clothes made in sweatshops. "The economics aren't there for people to care," Bellos told me. "Pollution is the cheapest way to do business."

With Stony Creek Colors, Bellos wants to prove that growing, producing, and using natural indigo is actually a smart, and profitable, business practice.

Bellos's background is very un-fashion. She grew up on Long Island, New York, in an old farmhouse in the forest. Her mother was an artist. Her father studied forestry and worked as a carpenter. "I played in the wetlands or in the woods," she said. "I've always been captivated by the environment."

She went to Cornell University, where she studied natural resource management, and North Carolina State University—the same school Natalie Chanin attended. Her first job, at an investment firm in Washington, DC, was to study how the company could invest—or put money into—projects or other businesses and earn big profits. But she quickly realized that sort of work didn't suit her. She quit and moved to Nashville, where her older sister, Alesandra, lived and worked as an artist.

They decided to launch their own small business, which would be sustainable, meaning not harmful to the environment. It was called Artisan Natural Dyeworks, and it was a dye house that worked with independent designers, including Natalie Chanin. The sisters learned how to make dye by reading books, and by experimenting. As successful as their company was, hand-dyeing fabric wasn't going to seriously improve "what I saw as the sustainability crisis in the industry," Bellos said. Artisan Natural Dyeworks was too small a company to effect major change on fashion's enormous problems, like mass pollution. So, in 2012, Bellos founded Stony Creek Colors, named for her small farm outside of Nashville. Stony Creek Colors was a bigger company, with bigger goals.

When I went to see Bellos, in the summer of 2016, she was the only person in the United States growing indigo on an industrial scale. Her biggest client was Cone Mills' White Oak factory in Greensboro, North Carolina—the one-hundred-year old mill that had been Levi's first major denim supplier. With her deal with Cone Mills, Bellos could afford to grow more indigo as well as open a factory.

At first look, using natural dyes seems to be more

expensive than synthetics, because it costs more to farm indigo in a field than it does to make synthetic indigo in a laboratory. But there are other expenses not included in calculating the true cost of synthetic indigo, like the environmental damage and the health issues.

A handful of Chinese manufacturers produce most synthetic indigo today, and for it they use a chemical called aniline. The Environmental Protection Agency classifies aniline as a Group B2, probable human carcinogen, meaning it may cause cancer. And the US Centers for Disease Control and Prevention has declared aniline "very toxic" to creatures and plants that live in water. Recent reports state that two-thirds of aniline on the fabric winds up in lakes, rivers, and other waterways; on workers; and in the air that workers breathe. The remaining third stays in the denim jeans, jackets, and skirts sold in stores.

It takes money to clean up environmental damage or to treat ill people—whether it's the government who covers it (funded by the taxes we pay), or directly out of our pockets (medical insurance and medical bills). Synthetic indigo is another example of the "false economy" that Maria Cornejo described. Companies using synthetic indigo *seem* to be saving money, and making more profits. But, in truth, when you add up all the other expenses, such as environmental damage and human illness, it actually costs much, *much* more for all of us.

- - -

Bellos suggested we go visit the fields in Greenbrier, a half-hour drive from her office. The fields were indeed muddy. The soil was clay-like and somewhat sandy. She didn't know if it was organic or not. Bellos doesn't own the fields, so she can't control what's done when she's not farming them, and there could be leftover chemical fertilizers or pesticides in the soil. But *her* operation is organic—she does not use chemical fertilizers or pesticides. Which means the soil is healthier after she grows her indigo in the fields.

Bellos's farmers grow three varieties of indigo: one from Japan called *Persicaria tinctoria,* and two tropical ones, *Indigofera suffruticosa* and *Indigofera tinctoria.*

The Japanese plants were hip high, dark green, and bushy, like giant basil. The air smelled pungent and sweet. The dye, Bellos explained, is in the leaves. She plucked a couple and handed them to me. I stuck them in my notebook; as they dried, they turned the same blue-black as her fingernails. Some of the Japanese plants were flowering. The blooms were a bright pink.

On the next field were the two tropical varieties. One was taller—up to my belly button—and gangly. The second was shorter and small leafed. Butterflies, ladybugs, and red wasps, which eat other bugs, buzzed around us. "Honeybees love it too," Bellos said. Generally, pests find indigo bitter and leave it alone. "Insects don't come back if it doesn't taste good!"

Tennessee has long been a tobacco state. But the number of Americans who smoke cigarettes has dropped a lot in recent years. So there is less need for tobacco farming.

This is good news for the Earth. Tobacco requires huge amounts of chemicals such as herbicides and fungicides, which kill weeds and disease. And tobacco plants suck nutrients from the soil. To grow tobacco plants in the same fields, year after year, farmers must dump heavy doses of nitrogen fertilizer—a chemical vitamin shot of sorts—in the soil. All these chemicals boost the energy of the soil immediately, and the plants do grow well. But over-planting and over-fertilizing the soil weakens it dramatically in the long term. And weak soil—like a weak human—is vulnerable to disease and weeds. So the fields must be treated with *more* herbicide and pesticide, which further wounds the soil.

Indigo is a legume, like soy. It needs far less fertilizer. In fact, the two tropical varieties require *zero* fertilizer; they naturally put nitrogen back into the earth, making it healthier and stronger than before.

Bellos had no trouble getting farmers to participate—they needed work, since tobacco farming was disappearing, and indigo is far easier to grow than tobacco. Natural indigo is lifting farming towns out of poverty as well as "nourishing the soil," Bellos said.

We drove about fifteen minutes to Springfield, to see her "factory"—a redbrick warehouse built in the 1950s to store tobacco. The factory's last owner, the American Snuff Company, had closed it, and laid off all the workers. The closing "was an economic disaster for the area," Bellos said. She decided to reopen the building—to rightshore, in a sense.

We walked downstairs to the parking lot out back. There were bales of indigo piled up next to a dumpster-like container called an extractor, which was filled with water. The indigo leaves are loaded into the extractor and soak for a few hours. The inky liquid is pumped into an enormous stainless-steel vat, where it is transformed into dye. Bellos showed me a plastic tub filled with processed indigo juice. It smelled like cat pee. When I said this, she laughed.

"We are producing nowhere near what the market wants," she said. Therefore, she plans to keep adding fields, and expanding her output. And if all goes well, she hopes "there will be more companies like us in ten years," she told me. "We'll see."

The best jeans today are made in Kojima, a small town in southwest Japan.

Why?

Because Kojima artisans weave the finest denim, and practice the finest craftsmanship, in the jeans business.

Kojima jeans are made with care.

So respected is Kojima's denim, each time I mention it to anybody who works in the jeans business, everyone—and I mean *everyone*—professes love for the fabric and declares that it is their *dream* to go see the weaving and dyeing process in person.

Japanese passion for American blue jeans began in the 1940s, when American troops stationed in Asia wore them when on leave in Tokyo. Rock 'n' roll star Elvis Presley's look in the 1950s—dark blue Levi's, which he cuffed at the bottom, and a denim work shirt—made jeans even cooler. With a cultural obsession for quality, the Japanese considered American-woven denim to be the best.

In 1965, Kotaro Ozaki, of Maruo Clothing, a manufacturer based in Kojima, decided to steer his company into jeans production. But not just any sort of blue jeans. These would be knockoffs, or copies, of American jeans, made of American denim.

Ozaki launched two brands with American-sounding names: Big John, for men, and Betty Smith, for women. Maruo jeans looked American, and they were made of American denim, but they were for the Japanese consumer.

In 1972, Kurabo, a mill in nearby Kurashiki, began weaving denim—a first for Japan. More brands cropped up, all with American-sounding names, like Bison and Big

Stone. Kojima became known as the Holy Land of Jeans.

Today, Kojima is a jeans tourism center. Visitors can take a bus with denim-covered seats from the Kojima train station to the center of town. There you can visit a jeans museum and walk down "Jeans Street," which has American-looking jeans shops and snack bars selling "blue jean" ice cream. I got a scoop on a cone. To me, it tasted like Pixy Stix.

Kojima's star brand today is Momotaro Jeans, a line started in 2006 and named for the Japanese fairy tale about a boy born from a peach and raised by a childless couple. Each year, Momotaro only produces forty-five thousand pairs of jeans made of machine-woven denim, all dyed with natural indigo. This is a very small amount, given the industry puts out a total of six billion pairs of jeans each year. These jeans are Momotaro's version of ready-to-wear—jeans you can buy in a store, and wear right away.

Momotaro also has a couture version of jeans—the ones you pay for, then have to wait, since they are made specifically for you. How special are these jeans? The cotton is the finest in the world, the dye is natural indigo, and the denim is woven on an antique weaving machine, called a loom, that is run by hand. We went to the Momotaro shop on Jeans Street, where the loom is located, to watch a demonstration.

Kazuki Ikeda, a handsome twenty-six-year-old man in a tailored denim suit, blue shirt, blue necktie, and polished shoes, stood at the loom. It was strung with two sets of yarn, both horizontally and vertically—imagine how a guitar is strung, but hundreds of strings, set to the width of the loom, which was about three feet.

To weave the fabric, Ikeda pushed forward a frame-shaped mechanism called "the beater" through the first set of horizontal and vertical yarn. He took the shuttle, which is a small oblong bobbin wound with more yarn, and slid it through. Then he pulled the beater back toward him hard twice—*thunk, thunk*—to make sure the shuttle yarn was tight against the previously woven section. The loom made a loud clunking noise as the first set of horizontal and vertical yarns shifted back and the second set shifted forward. He pushed the beater forward again, zipped through the shuttle, pulled it back: *thunk, thunk*. Then the loom shifted back to the first set of horizontal and vertical yarn: *clunk*. And on and on it went: beater forward; shuttle through; beater back; *thunk, thunk; clunk;* beater forward; shuttle through; beater back; *thunk, thunk; clunk.*

Ikeda had trained for five years with a master weaver to learn the technique. To get the weave right, he must apply the same pressure with each movement. During an eight-hour workday, he can weave seventy centimeters (or about two feet) of denim. A bolt is fifty meters (or fifty-four yards—half a football field). It takes three months for him to weave one bolt of cloth.

Each year, Momotaro produces twenty pairs of jeans with this denim. "We wanted to create the ultimate jeans," Momotaro's general manager, Tatsushi Tabuchi, told me. "Japan has a tradition of hand weaving," and working on the kimono loom "preserves that technique," he said. The quality is clear. The surface of the thread is round—mass-production machines crush that roundness—and there is a fluffy feel to it. The jeans are solidly made, handsome, and will last for years and years. Despite the fact that these jeans cost 200,000 yen, or roughly $2,000, a pair, there is a wait list. For a while, Momotaro stopped taking orders because, Tabuchi said, "We couldn't keep up."

The Japanese proved that high-quality, profitable, and desirable jeans can be made following the slow fashion model. What could be done about finishing? Surely, in our world of rapid technological advancement, there must be a way to stop the horrors I saw when I visited the denim sweatshop in Ho Chi Minh City, Vietnam.

Denim industry experts José Vidal and his nephew Enrique Silla, based in Valencia, Spain, posed themselves the same question and invented a cleaner, safer process. Called Jeanologia (pronounced "Jee-no-LO-jee-ah"), it is a three-step system: lasers, which replace sandblasting, hand-sanding, and bleaching; ozone, which fades fabrics without chemicals; and e-Flow, a washing system that uses microscopic "nanobubbles" to reduce water usage. The Jeanologia system can decrease energy consumption by 33 percent, chemicals by 67 percent, and if implemented most efficiently, water usage by 71 percent—or, as the company proudly boasts, to one glass of water per pair of jeans. Of the six billion pairs of jeans manufactured and finished in 2018, about 30 percent went through at least some part of the Jeanologia system.

Enrique Silla, the company's chief executive, led me to the lab to see the system in action. In the laser room, a young man pulled brand-new, untouched jeans onto the legs of a half-mannequin in a transparent cabin. His partner stood nearby at a computer control panel and launched the process: The lasers went down the face of the jeans—at least that's what I thought was happening, since the beams were invisible—and clouds of blue smoke puffed as distress patterns emerged. In ten or eleven seconds, it was all over: The jeans were as faded and destroyed as my old shrink-to-fit Levi's 501s after three years of wear. "Technology is the way forward," Silla said. "It's cleaner and healthier."

In the next room, Silla showed me a dryer-like tumbler called the G2 Cube that uses ozone to fade jeans. Using ozone in finishing is "like putting a garment in the sun for a month, except we can do it in twenty minutes," and use a fraction of the energy or water the old process required, Silla said.

Finally, we visited the washroom, outfitted with e-Flow: a machine that washes jeans with bubbles so microscopic, they add up to one million per cubic centimeter—the size of a sugar cube. With the traditional wash system, you soak the entire garment. Think about when your clothes are washed at home, and how they come out of the washing machine sopping wet. The nanobubbles are like a fog—they only moisten the surface of the denim. I stuck my hand in the machine. It felt like steam, but cold, with a bit of pressure and a little prickling. "Nanobubbles do the softening, tinting, and stonewash without the stones, all at once," Silla said. The water can be recycled for thirty days. "We are not at the zero water stage yet," he said. "But we are getting there."

When I was in Ho Chi Minh City, I toured a Jeanologia-equipped washhouse to see the process on an industrial scale. What a difference from the dirty, noisy sweatshop I had visited earlier in the day, where I had witnessed workers hand-sanding and machine-distressing jeans in the sweltering heat. At the modern washhouse, the spacious glass-walled rooms were bright, clean, quiet, and air-conditioned: The machines, as well as the workers, needed a steady cool temperature to avoid overheating. Jeanologia had "totally transformed production," Silla said.

I saw what he meant. In the e-Flow washroom, the floor wasn't flooded, workers didn't need rubber boots, and their hands weren't blue. It was clean, dry, and quiet. In the dry process room, the whiskering fade pattern on the front of the jeans was achieved by ozone, not chemicals. That room too was clean, dry, and quiet. In the distressing rooms, lasers moved invisibly down the jeans, the wisp of fine blue dust sucked up by the vacuum system. No dust. No noise. No health concerns. The factory processed 25,000 to 30,000 pairs of jeans a day—about half of what the big Chinese factories churn out. There was no frenetic grabbing and flinging of jeans, no screeching sanders, no unbearable heat, no stress.

I asked about job loss—an argument I hear all the time from those who are against the use of factory robots—since the lasers were a robot-like automation. "Eventually everything will be robotic," Silla said. But instead of firing workers who used to do the finishing by hand, this factory retrains them to use "more sophisticated machinery, or to manage," Silla said. Again, like I'd heard at English Fine Cottons in Manchester and in the Carolinas, while there were fewer jobs, the work was safer, less tiring, and better paying. Workers at the Jeanologia plant would not be hurriedly hand-sanding jeans, and inhaling fibers and synthetic indigo dust.

"A cleaner industry," Silla told me proudly.

His aim was to get the major brands, such as Gap, H&M, Zara, Uniqlo, PVH, VF Corp, and Levi's, to use such a system in their jeans finishing. They produce most of the six billion pairs of jeans we buy and wear every year.

"If we transform the way these people produce," Silla said, "that would be immense."

With Levi's, there was hope.

After decades of greedy, careless, and irresponsible decisions that shattered small towns and nearly bankrupted the company, in 2011, Levi's made what may turn out to be its smartest business move in more than a century: The company hired Chip Bergh, a lanky, fifty-three-year-old former US Army captain, as the new chief executive. Bergh had a lot of experience in global business: He had spent twenty-eight years at Procter & Gamble, the megacorporation that includes such brands as Tide detergent, Crest toothpaste, and Pampers diapers. Bergh promised he would "change the culture" at Levi's. The days of decisions made for short-term gains were over.

At the time, Levi's research and development center—

the place where they experiment with fabrics, dyes, and finishes—was located in Turkey. Why? Because doing business in Turkey was cheaper than in San Francisco.

But this setup was exactly what Maria Cornejo meant when she talked about the "false economy"—or fake savings—in fashion: Cutting costs by putting offices in a cheaper place, like Turkey, then wasting money traveling from the company's headquarters to that cheap place and back.

And that's what happened with Levi's. Whenever the design team in San Francisco wanted to try something new, or the lab technicians in Turkey wanted to show managers what they'd come up with, someone would have to hop on a plane or FedEx a sample halfway around the world. It might have appeared on paper that the company was saving money by having the research lab in Turkey rather than San Francisco, but the calculations didn't take into account all the expenses—the plane tickets, hotels, meals, taxis, travel time, days off to recover from the exhaustion or illness from all that travel, the pollution generated by the travel and shipping, and so on.

In 2012, Bergh decided it was time to bring innovation back home to San Francisco. But he didn't just reshore it; he rightshored it. He opened Eureka Innovation Lab, a new high-tech research and development center, in a former grain mill at the foot of Telegraph Hill in San

Francisco, a five-minute walk from Levi's global head-quarters. He put American-born denim expert Bart Sights, who ran the center in Turkey, in charge.

Today at the Eureka Lab, a team of thirty technicians "tests jeans for strength, stretch and recovery, durability, water repellency, how the garment would react in a home laundry—all sorts of things," Sights explained to me as we toured the two-story building.

On the cement floor lay a dozen pairs of Levi's in various states of distress—some washed, some faded, some worn out and tattered. These were "prototypes"—one-of-a-kind examples to see what the jeans look like with different treatments. "We need to be able to ensure that if we make one, we can make a million of them," he said.

Across the room was a mini-factory with cone-shaped spools of thread in Levi's basic colors of navy, black, white, and gold; bolts of denim leaning against a wall; and nine seamstresses at machines, sewing jeans for Sights's team to test.

After jeans are sewed, they are finished so they look worn and fashionable. There are sophisticated processing machines throughout the Eureka Innovation Lab, including industrial washers and dryers. In a small back room called "the physical testing lab," I spied a Jeanologia machine. At the time, the lab was testing the system. Four months later, Levi's announced it was introducing

Jeanologia's laser distressing systems throughout its supply chain. Levi's, the world's largest jeans company, was going to finish its jeans in a cleaner, safer manner, improving conditions for both the planet and for workers.

"This," Bergh said, "is the future of jeans."

PART THREE

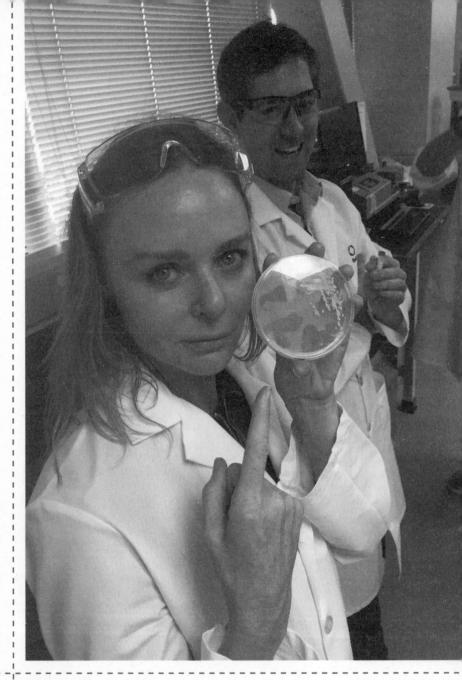

Stella McCartney in the lab of Bolt Threads in San Francisco.
© 2016 by Stephane Jaspar.

SEVEN

WE CAN WORK IT OUT

On a rainy March morning in Paris, hundreds of editors, retailers, and influencers stepped out of Ubers and taxis in front of the Palais Garnier opera house and dashed up the theater's old, wet stone steps.

They were there to see British designer Stella McCartney's Fall-Winter 2017–2018 women's wear show.

At 9:45, the lights were turned down, and for a moment, the crowd hushed.

Then the thumping music of rapper Princess Nokia blasted over the speakers. McCartney's models marched by in caramel-colored wool jumpsuits, gray wool flannel pantsuits with crisp white cotton shirts, and viscose dresses printed with images of wild horses, blue skies and clouds.

What the audience couldn't see as the models whizzed by: The wool came from a sustainable sheep farm in New Zealand; the viscose, a wood-pulp-based synthetic fabric, was made from Swedish wood certified by the Forest Stewardship Council; and the cotton was a heritage variety farmed organically in Egypt.

Many fashion brands present their new collections during Paris fashion week. But only McCartney calls herself a "conscious designer." She does all that she can, in business and life, to respect nature and humanity.

McCartney is a lifelong vegetarian who has always designed and produced clothes and accessories that are "animal-free," meaning no leather, no fur. Her supply chain is transparent, which means she makes information available on how her clothes are made. She can tell you from which farm the wool in her suits comes—she might be able to even tell you from which sheep. She can tell you in what field the cotton in that shirt was grown. She makes sure the people who produce her fashion are paid a living wage, work in safe factories, and are treated well. Her stores are built with recyclable materials and many are powered ecologically—with wind power, for example.

And since 2013, McCartney's company has produced an Environmental Profit and Loss report (EP&L). Every company puts out a profit and loss report, which is exactly as it sounds: The company adds up how much money it made ("income"), and how much money it spent ("expenses"), and then it sees if the total is a "profit" (they made money), or a "loss" (they lost money).

The EP&L does the same thing, except that, rather than measuring income and expenses, it measures the brand's impact on the environment. In other words, McCartney tracks how everything the company does—"from farms to finished products," as she explained it—touches or affects nature. Then she studies these effects, and figures out how to lessen harm or destruction, and, if possible, help nature.

By using the EP&L, McCartney can run a business that's better for people and for the environment.

McCartney is the perfect person to lead the fight for a greener, cleaner fashion industry.

She is the daughter of Paul McCartney, who was one of the members of the British rock band the Beatles. When she was a young girl, the family lived on an organic farm in Sussex, England, and her parents were famously vegetarian and pro-animal rights. They never ate meat, or wore leather or fur. In the 1980s, McCartney's late mother, the American-born photographer Linda Eastman McCartney, wrote best-selling vegetarian cookbooks and, in 1991, she launched a prepared vegetarian food line that remains successful today. (Continuing the tradition, McCartney too is raising her four children, with her husband, Alasdhair Willis, as anti-leather, anti-fur vegetarians.)

During her childhood in the 1970s, McCartney was

a tomboy, who rode her pony through the English countryside and played in streams. But she also loved fashion.
When she was twelve or thirteen, she sewed a jacket out
of fake suede—the first garment she designed and produced on her own. As a teenager in the 1980s, McCartney
interned for top fashion designers in Paris and in London.
In the early 1990s, she studied fashion design at Central
Saint Martins College of Art and Design in London. In her
spare time, she worked for her father's tailor, and learned
how to cut and sew a suit. After finishing college in 1995,
she started a small company, and made pretty slip dresses
from antique silk and lace she bought in flea markets.

Two years later, French luxury ready-to-wear brand
Chloé (pronounced "KLO-ay") in Paris offered her a job
as chief designer. She said yes, but with one condition:
She would not use leather or fur.

"Killing animals is the most destructive thing you can
do in the fashion industry," she told me. "The tanneries,
the chemicals, the deforestation, the use of landmass and
grain and water, the cruelty."

After four years at Chloé in Paris, she left to start her
own brand, based in London. Gucci Group (now known
as Kering), a corporate luxury group made up of several
brands, bought half her company; she owned the other
half. Again, she insisted: No leather, no fur.

Gucci executives agreed to her conditions for her
brand. But they weren't sure how it was going to work

out. After all, leather goods, such as handbags and wallets, are how luxury brands like Gucci, Louis Vuitton, and Chanel make big money. The price is marked up 20 to 25 times production costs: If it costs $100 to make a handbag, the company sells it for $2,000 to $2,500. Leather goods are fashion's money machine. And fashion executives believed that no one would pay big money for leather goods made out of fake leather, or out of fabric.

On the day we met, at a small hotel near her home in London, McCartney showed me her handbag. It was made of synthetic leather and lined with recycled fake suede. As I turned it over in my hands and ran my fingertips across the grain, she asked, "Really, does anyone know it's not leather?"

Not me, I thought.

Five years after she started her company, it was profitable—meaning she was making money, rather than losing it. And a "significant" portion of her sales were accessories—the handbags, wallets, and shoes executives told her no one would buy if they weren't made of real leather. "I've proven that wrong," she said.

After her no-fur, no-leather success, McCartney decided to look carefully at the other materials she used in her fashion line, to see which ones were the most highly polluting and could be eliminated. She zeroed in on one: polyvinyl chloride, known as PVC.

PVC is one of the most popular plastics today. Cling

wrap, drinking straws, credit cards, strollers, toys, artificial Christmas trees, Scotch tape, and plumbing pipes are all made of PVC. In fashion, it is used for transparent shoe heels, vinyl raincoats, patent-leather shoes, and the flexible tubing inside handbag handles. But PVC is known to cause cancer. And when PVC biodegrades in landfills, it releases poisons into soil and water. In 2010, McCartney banned all use of PVC at her company.

"Taking PVC out was a huge thing for us," she said. "I'd say: 'Let's do a clear heel!' PVC, PVC, PVC. 'Let's do sequins!' There are two sequins in the world without PVC. There are millions of gorgeous sequins, but they have PVC."

By 2016, all Kering brands had stopped using PVC. For McCartney, it was a big win.

McCartney wouldn't have been able to put any of these big pro-environment changes into effect at her company had it not been for the help of her sustainability and ethical trade chief Claire Bergkamp.

Like McCartney, Bergkamp has always loved fashion. And like McCartney, she grew up in the countryside, far from fashion capitals. Bergkamp is an American, born and raised in Helena, Montana. She subscribed to *Vogue* throughout her youth ("I can tell you, in Montana, I was a freak!") and shopped in Idaho malls when on soccer team trips (there were no decent malls in Helena). She knew early on, however, that her interest lay more in "what it means to wear something," she told me, than about trends, or shopping.

Bergkamp graduated from Emerson College in Boston in 2007 with a bachelor's degree in costume design, and spent four years in Los Angeles working in film and television. Then she decided to enroll in the London College of Fashion, to get a second, more advanced degree—called a master's—with a focus on sustainability. Shortly after she completed the two-year program, she landed a job at Stella McCartney in London. Her assignment: to help make the company more sustainable.

It was Bergkamp's job to set up the Environmental Profit and Loss (EP&L) report—the system that measures how the brand's supply chain affects—or "impacts"—the environment. The supply chain is the path that a product takes as it is made: In the case of fashion, this includes cotton fields, sheep ranches, laboratories where synthetic fabrics are developed and produced, the factories where clothes are sewed, and so on, all the way to the store floor.

The EP&L looks at several major ways a company can damage the environment, including air pollution, water pollution, water consumption, and waste. Once the company knows its impact, it can change its practices for the better.

For McCartney, the EP&L spotted a few damaging practices.

One category to study was the company's raw materials—the basics employed to make clothing, like cotton, wool, silk, polyester, and cashmere. This last material raised some concerns. Cashmere is made of a super-soft fiber combed off goats in Mongolia and spun into yarn. That yarn is used to produce sweaters, dresses, scarves.

McCartney's EP&L showed that the brand-new, or "virgin," cashmere she used for her clothes caused the most damage to the environment of all her raw materials. It takes four goats to get enough fiber to make one cashmere sweater. By comparison, the wool of one sheep makes *five* sweaters.

For centuries, cashmere had been considered a luxury product: It was precious, rare, and expensive. It took time to raise and care for the goats, and comb and spin the fiber. The yarn was extra soft to touch—it felt like a cloud. To own a cashmere sweater or scarf was extremely special.

But in the 1990s, two things happened to make cashmere more common, less special, and more environmentally destructive.

First, Mongolia, the Asian country where most cashmere goats are raised, switched from a communist economy, where the government strictly controlled business decisions, to one that was more like a capitalist economy, where businesses are relatively free to do as they please.

At the same time, fast-fashion began selling inexpensive, low-quality cashmere sweaters for less than $70 apiece.

These sweaters weren't as thick and soft as the expensive, luxury versions. And they certainly didn't last as long—your elbow would poke through the knit after one season's wear. But they were so cheap, you could always buy another one. And consumers did. A lot. Fast-fashion started producing and selling *millions* of cashmere sweaters. The demand for cashmere sweaters exploded.

Herders in Mongolia's mountains increased the number of goats from five million in the 1990s to twenty-one million today—all on the same amount of land. Goats eat everything, and eat nonstop. They pull up grass by its roots. Because there were four times more goats grazing on the same amount of land, by 2017, 70 percent of Mongolia's grasslands were destroyed, and the fields were turning into desert. If fashion's demand for cashmere keeps growing at the same rate, Mongolia will have to increase the number of goats to *forty-four million* by 2025. The country will become like a giant desert, and the goats—and the people—will have nothing left to eat.

Because of this environmental destruction, Stella

McCartney switched in 2016 from virgin (or new) cashmere to "regenerated" cashmere, which is cashmere made of production waste, such as the extra bits that fall to the factory floor. Regenerated cashmere is 92 percent less damaging to the environment than virgin cashmere.

How do these pro-environment policies change the way McCartney makes fashion?

Take the clothes in her March 2017 fashion show at the Paris opera house. The flannel suits were made of wool from a ranch on New Zealand's South Island, where the sheep are allowed to roam freely. "Happy sheep produce better quality wool," Claire Bergkamp said with a laugh. The cotton came from organically farmed fields. The viscose for the dresses came from responsibly forested trees. The clothes were cut and sewed in a Hungarian factory where workers earn a living wage in clean, safe conditions.

McCartney's stores in Great Britain run on wind power. The Dallas store has solar panels. The one in Costa Mesa, California, has skylights, reducing the reliance on electric lighting. In London, at 23 Old Bond Street in Mayfair, shelves are made of recycled wood, the wallpaper is a papier-mâché of office printouts, and the air is run through a filtration system, removing 95 percent of pollutants. "It's the cleanest air in London!" McCartney told me.

"We take conscious design throughout the entire company," she explained during our first meeting in Notting Hill. "Every single piece of paper, every single bag, is all recycled and recyclable." She handed me one of her shopping bags: It read on the bottom, *Made of recycled materials.*

"Yes, I know that the moment I create a product, any product, I'm in some way creating a footprint," she admitted. "You can't pretend that's not the case. But I always try to find a solution."

One person who offers solutions is Swiss business-woman Nina Marenzi, founder of The Sustainable Angle, a company that promotes the research and sales of sustainable fabrics and materials.

At her studio in London, we were surrounded by a dozen garment racks, each full of hundreds of examples of cool new fabrics. Like a fake-leather canvas called Pellemela, which is made of apple juice waste. And a squishy brown suede made of mushrooms. And a beautiful red "leather" that felt creamy and smelled sweet, like a fruit pie. "It's made of rhubarb!" Marenzi said with a laugh.

There was Sally Fox's colored cotton, in shades of green, brown, and beige.

"Imagine how much money you could save in the

dyeing process if cotton was already colored," Marenzi said.

There was cotton cloth with a waterproof coating of rubber from the Amazon forest. "This helps local tribes," Marenzi explained as she handed it to me. "They collect the latex from rubber trees and get some income, rather than chopping down the trees and converting the land to agriculture," meaning traditional farming, with big fields. There was a white crepe (pronounced "craype"), a thin, soft fabric with a wrinkly texture, made of Orange Fiber, a fake silk invented by two Italian students as a way to reuse 700,000 tons of orange juice waste—like rinds and pulp—in Italy each year. The Italian luxury brand Salvatore Ferragamo has used Orange Fiber to make shirts, dresses, pants, and scarves.

"A majority of fashion's problems could be solved at the design process," Marenzi said.

Yet, as cool as they are, Marenzi has to fight to get these fabrics the orders they need to keep going. "The big firms all say they have no budgets for sustainability," she told me, sounding frustrated. That is a common excuse. For executives in the fashion business, short-term profits are more important than long-term good works. Which reminded me of what Nashville indigo farmer Sarah Bellos told me: "Pollution is the cheapest way to do business."

- - -

McCartney's most important, and lasting, act in sustainability is her support of start-ups, as new companies are called.

One such brand is Modern Meadow, an American high-tech company that scientifically grows animal-free leather-like material in a laboratory.

Lab-grown leather-like material, also called biofabrication, is seen as a safe, clean replacement for fake leathers, which are usually made of petroleum (the crude oil pumped from the Earth's core, also used for gasoline) and treated with PVC. Lab-grown leather-like materials are also a good way to shrink traditional leather's harmful supply chain—from industrial farming of animals for the skins to the toxic chemicals used to treat the skins—and to cut waste. With biofabrication, there are no leftovers— you grow only what you need. And it is animal-free, so vegans can wear it. All of this is good for the environment, which we must consider in everything we do, to stop or slow down climate change.

"You use less water, less electricity, and no landmass," Modern Meadow's Chief Creative Officer Suzanne Lee told me. "I am very excited for the day that I can have my entire store offerings made out of lab-grown leather."

On a sunny summer morning in 2017, I visited Modern Meadow's headquarters in Brooklyn, New York.

In the laboratory, scientists in black coats watched over bubbling bioreactors and trays of test tubes. "They think they are lab ninjas," Lee said with a laugh.

The ninjas practice "complex biotechnology," she said. Biotechnology is the science of modifying living organisms for human purposes. In this case, the process is based on a relatively easy notion to understand: It's the same system as "how you brew beer," Lee said. "But instead of beer, we're making collagen—the protein found in skin."

We walked back to her office so she could show me a few samples of Modern Meadow's material.

The first was round and thin, like a tortilla, black, and slightly rough.

"We call this one 'elephant,'" Lee said.

I felt it with my fingertips and held it up to my nose.

"It's like real leather," I said.

She nodded.

She handed me a second tortilla-size swatch, also black, but thinner and craggy, like rhino hide.

The third black tortilla was soft and fine, similar to Italian glove leather.

"Every month these look different," Lee said as she put them away. "We are learning so much at every step of the process." I spotted a sewing machine in the corner of her office. She uses it to test the material—"to make sure you can stitch and construct with it like traditional materials," she said. Eventually, Modern Meadow's material will be sold commercially.

The company is also developing liquid leather-like material, to glue seams together or to pour into molds, and growing material in specific shapes.

"What does the car seat of the future look like?" Lee asked me. "Maybe it's stitched. Maybe it's not. You can grow [a car seat or handbag] to shape, instead of cutting and sewing it.

"We don't want to replace traditional craftsmanship," she cautioned. "But we do want to show that there is an alternative . . . [that] we can go so far beyond the use of traditional leather."

Another company McCartney supports is Bolt Threads, a high-tech start-up in San Francisco that produces silk in a laboratory.

The Chinese began to produce silk for clothing five thousand years ago. For centuries, the Chinese kept the method of making silk a secret, and anyone found guilty of disclosing it was sentenced to death. But in the thirteenth century, the explorer Marco Polo brought silk—and the knowledge to make it—back to Europe, on the trade route called the Silk Road. Italy and France soon became silk production capitals too.

Silk is created through the process of sericulture, or silkworm farming. Silkworms are not worms, but caterpillars of the Bombyx mori moth. Today, the Bombyx mori caterpillar is raised on farms in China, Thailand, and India, where it eats Mulberry tree leaves and increases its bodyweight ten thousand times in its four-week lifespan to about the size of an adult thumb.

After four moltings, the caterpillar spins a two-inch-long waterproof cocoon, ejecting liquid silk at about a foot a minute. In the silk-making process, cocoons are steamed to kill the caterpillar, washed by hand in hot water to remove a gummy substance called sericin that holds it together, and unwound on a reeling machine, which spools the silk filaments on a bobbin. The work is fast, and the water is filthy, smelly, and very hot to the touch. Usually five to eight silk filaments are spun together to create a thread.

The problem in the silk process for McCartney was the killing of the silkworm. This practice is against McCartney's belief that animals shouldn't be harmed for fashion. By growing silk in a laboratory, Bolt was offering an animal-free alternative.

The science behind Bolt's silk is similar to Modern Meadow's leather-like material: DNA is introduced to yeast, and is programmed to produce silk. The yeast goes through a chemical process where it is turned into pure silk. During the process, the laboratory will smell like baking bread. The silk is colored with textile dyes and spun on a series of spindles, each one whirring faster and pulling tighter to crystallize the fiber and build the yarn's structure. Bolt calls their lab-grown yarn Microsilk. By touch and sight, I could not tell it wasn't natural silk.

Stella McCartney has used Bolt Threads's Microsilk to make dresses for museum exhibits. She is also using Bolt's second biotech material, Mylo, a fake leather made of mycelium, the underground root structure of mushrooms, to make handbags, wallets, and shoes. McCartney will have clothing items and accessories made of Microsilk and Mylo in her stores soon.

Bolt Threads and Modern Meadow are giving McCartney, and the rest of the fashion industry, sustainable alternatives to traditional raw materials, such as leather and silk. The creation and production of these high-tech materials are safer and cleaner for the environment, and for workers. No animals are killed in the process, which pleases animal rights activists and vegetarians. And it's a modern response to all the damage the fashion industry causes to the Earth and to humanity.

For McCartney, being sustainable is "the most modern thing that you can do."

Patagonia's Worn Wear Wagon.
© 2014 by Erin Feinblatt.

EIGHT

AROUND AND AROUND WE GO

Seven months after my first visit to Première Vision, the world's largest fabric fair at an enormous convention center outside of Paris, I was back there again. This time I went to see Evrnu, a Seattle-based start-up that takes old cotton T-shirts and jeans, breaks the material down to molecules, and turns the molecules back into new cotton yarn for fabric.

What Evrnu does is known as "circularity." Since the moment Richard Arkwright opened his first cotton mill in Manchester 250 years ago, and kicked off the Industrial Revolution, we have been consuming mass-manufactured products in a linear manner, like a timeline: The product is made; we buy the product; we use the product; we throw away the product. Then we start again: A new product is made, bought, used, and thrown in the trash. And over and over. It's a straight line, with a beginning, middle, and end. Could be a car. Could be a shirt. Could be a toy. In the end, it winds up in the garbage.

In a circular system, products are continually recycled,

reborn, and reused. A product is made; we buy the product; we use the product; the product is recycled; we buy it in its new form; we use it; it is recycled again; and on and on, in a circle.

Say the product is a shirt. In the linear world, the shirt is made; you buy the shirt; you wear the shirt; and when you are tired of it, or it's worn out, you throw it away, and it goes to landfill.

But in a circular world, thanks to Evrnu, the shirt is made; you buy the shirt; you wear the shirt; Evrnu collects the shirt; regenerates the cotton; a new shirt or dress is made; someone buys it; wears it; it gets worn out; Evrnu collects it; and the cotton keeps on being useful. Nothing goes in the trash, and then to landfill.

Why is circularity so important? Because today, only 1 percent of our clothing is recycled. The rest is sent to landfill or is burned. Our landfills are *heaving* with clothes. We will eventually run out of places to bury all our old clothes. And if we continue to produce clothes with only new materials, our natural resources, such as soil and water, will soon be depleted. When we recycle clothes, there is less farming (for cotton), less grazing (for cashmere and wool), less drilling for petroleum (for polyester and nylon), less tree cutting (for rayon), and less water usage (for everything). Circularity saves the planet.

With all the innovation and creativity that exists today, why should anything go to waste?

Fashion industry veteran Stacy Flynn posed this same question to herself. And it propelled her to invent Evrnu, a regenerated cotton made of 100 percent post-consumer clothing—the clothes you throw away. Evrnu uses 98 percent less water than virgin cotton; produces 80 percent less greenhouse gas emissions than polyester, viscose, or elastane (i.e., spandex, Lycra); emits zero plastic microfibers; causes zero deforestation; and requires zero farmland.

And, as I saw at Flynn's stand at Première Vision, Evrnu cotton looks, feels, and wears like traditional cotton that has been produced in a linear manner—from field to form. You can't tell that Evrnu fabric is made of regenerated cotton.

Flynn is an old hand in the fashion business. Over the years, she has worked for such major brands as Target and Eddie Bauer. When she worked for Target, in the early 2000s, she would travel to China to visit the factories that made products for the retailer. Flynn said these factories were top-tier—clean, safe, run professionally. "You could eat off the floor," she told me. "I was like, 'China's lovely, China's pristine, we have no problems in China.'"

But when she returned to China in 2010, on behalf of a small American textile firm, and visited the factories it used, she saw the other side—the hidden side—of apparel manufacturing. These factories were not top-tier, like the ones Target contracted. Far from it.

"At ten o'clock at night we go into this facility. There's one light source in the center of the room. There are people sewing all over the place, in the dark. There's an area where they have fabric spread out and a skull-and-crossbones on the chemicals. A guy smoking right in front of it, where it says *Flammable*. I'm like, 'Where am I?' I backed into a wall, and it started crumbling. It was grim—the land of the living dead. All the rules were being broken. It opened my eyes to what low price does," she recalled. "Then I began adding up how many billions of yards of fabric I'd made up to that point in my career, and I became linked to the cause."

She returned to Seattle, went back to college, and earned a master's degree in business, focusing on sustainable systems.

During her studies, Flynn learned that 90 percent of all clothing is made from two fibers—polyester and cotton—and most of that clothing ends up in landfills.

"The design challenge was clear: Take the waste and turn it into high-quality new fiber," she said.

Forty-five and small, with a mop of soft blond curls and an energy so positive and vibrant, it could light up a Christmas tree, Flynn is the essence of American can-do. "If Stacy sets her mind to something, she'll make it happen," Stella McCartney's sustainability chief Claire Bergkamp told me. "You can be sure of that."

In fashion and apparel, Flynn said, "we fail to innovate on so many levels because we've been reliant on nineteenth-century equipment"—spinners, looms, sewing machines—"and the way we think about that equipment is with a twentieth-century mindset—that resources are infinite, that cash is the only thing that matters."

Flynn and her partner, industry veteran Christopher "Christo" Stanev, realized that they had to "find solutions that could change the system without asking consumers, brands, or makers to change too much at one time," she said.

In other words, baby steps.

They formed their company and set to unlocking the science that converts the cloth into a honey-like goo called cellulose. They run the goo through a machine called an extruder to turn the cellulose back into yarn. "Visualize making pasta," Flynn told me. "You start with dough, then you push the dough through a dial that makes the shape," like spaghetti. Except the goo becomes yarn. They named the product Evrnu, pronounced "ever new" but written in an abbreviation. "Like a license plate," she said.

She reached over to her display table and picked up a ball of shimmery white fluff.

It was made of 51 percent Evrnu and 49 percent

virgin—or new—cotton, she explained as she handed it to me.

I found myself compulsively stroking it.

"It's like petting a baby bunny," I said.

"I know, right?" she said, laughing.

One day, Flynn attended a conference at the Fashion Institute of Technology, a fashion university in New York. One of the conference speakers was Levi's innovation head, Paul Dillinger.

"And he said, 'Anyone who can figure out how to create a high-quality recycled cotton is going to basically be queen or king of the universe,'" Flynn recalled.

After Dillinger's speech, Flynn walked up to him, introduced herself, and handed him a sample.

"This is made from 100 percent regenerated post-consumer garment waste," she told him. It was a piece of Evrnu yarn, high-quality recycled cotton from fabric someone has once owned and thrown in the trash—just like Dillinger talked about in his speech.

He touched the sample.

"We need to talk," he said.

In 2016, Evrnu and Levi's unveiled the first two pairs of 501 jeans created with denim made of a blend of organic cotton and Evrnu. Dillinger called them "a little industrial miracle." Levi's hopes to soon be selling Evrnu 501s.

After Levi's came Stella McCartney. When I met Flynn at Première Vision in 2018, she showed me her first prototype for Stella McCartney: a four-inch square of black single-weave crepe, a thin, silky fabric with a wrinkly texture, made of 51 percent Evrnu and 49 percent cotton. It was handsome and looked like a fine silk crepe. McCartney was so happy with the swatch, she moved forward to develop the fabric with Evrnu in Italy. Flynn is also working with her former colleagues at Target to produce items with Evrnu for its stores.

The potential supply of raw materials for a company like Evrnu is endless. There are all the millions of clothes we throw away; in New York City alone, apparel and textiles make up more than 6 percent of all garbage, which equals nearly 200,000 tons a year.

There are the clothes we give away: Of the 15 percent of our clothes we donate—rather than throw in the trash—only about one-fifth actually goes to those in need. The rest are sold to for-profit textile recyclers, who turn the cloth into mattress stuffing, insulation, or rags. All of that waste can be used to make Evrnu.

Flynn can also take "preconsumer waste"—the scraps that fall on the factory floor during the manufacturing process. And "deadstock"—leftover clothes that don't sell and brands usually burn or shred.

"Christo and I have mapped this out for the next twenty

years. I'll be seventy-seven years old," Flynn said. "Then the kids can take it. When the kids that are in the world right now come to me and say, 'What did you do when you learned there was an environmental crisis?' I'm going to say, 'I changed the way I think and act, I fought like hell, and I influenced a whole bunch of other people to change the way they think and act. We didn't sit on the sidelines. Good luck.'"

Stacy Flynn has found a solution for cotton clothing waste. But what about synthetics, like polyester?

After all, more than 60 percent of all clothes contain polyester.

Unlike cotton, which humans have used for more than 7,000 years, polyester has a short history—less than 100 years.

Synthetic fabrics were invented in the 1930s, when American chemist Wallace Carothers, head of DuPont laboratories in Wilmington, Delaware, began experimenting with polymers—the molecular structure of plastic. Synthetic fabrics such as artificial silk, nylon, and neoprene (the thick stretchy material for wetsuits) are among the fabrics that came from his work. In 1941, British chemists John Rex Whinfield and James Tennant Dickson, of Manchester, built on Carothers's advances to create polyethylene terephthalate—also known as PET or PETE—the basis for polyester, Dacron, and Terylene.

Synthetics became popular during World War II, when cotton, wool, and silk were used for uniforms, parachutes, and bandages. Fashion companies used fabrics made of synthetics as a replacement. There were nylon stockings, polyester shirts, artificial silk dresses.

At first, like so many inventions, synthetics were considered a wonderful breakthrough and the perfect solution for a need at the time. But nearly a century on, it is clear that polyester and its cousins aren't so wonderful after all.

Polyester, the most popular synthetic fabric, is petroleum based; nearly seventy million barrels of crude oil, sourced by drilling in the Earth's core, are needed to make the polyester used for fabrics each year.

Cotton-polyester blended fabrics represent about one-third of all cloth produced today. Because no one had figured out how to separate the cotton and the polyester after the fabric's use, garments made of the blend could not be recycled. When these clothes came to the end of their life, people would throw them away, and they'd usually be sent to the dump. Polyester is not biodegradable.

Cyndi Rhoades, an American entrepreneur who has long lived in London, got to thinking about all that waste. And just like Stacy Flynn, Rhoades asked herself:

"Wouldn't it be smarter to put it back in the system?"

Meaning: Make polyester circular.

A decade on, Rhoades is doing just that, with a company she founded called Worn Again Technologies.

Worn Again has developed a process that separates polyester and cotton cellulose from polyester-cotton blend fabrics. It converts the polymers back into new polyester and the cotton cellulose back into cotton fiber (like Evrnu does). And this process is changing the way clothes are made, used, and made again. It is making fashion more circular.

Unlike Flynn, Rhoades was a stranger to fashion.

Born and raised in Columbus, Ohio, Rhoades moved to Los Angeles in the early 1990s and worked in music videos. She landed in London in 1993 for what she thought would be a three-month stay, and never went back. She kept producing music videos for rock bands and documentaries for British government agencies.

After reading a few books about the fashion industry, she decided she wanted to understand how fashion is made, and how to make the process more environmentally responsible. She wanted to do something to help "solve the textiles waste problem," she told me.

She thought that one solution could be "breaking down materials to their original components and putting them back together again," she said. Like Evrnu was doing with cotton, but instead doing it with polyester and with polyester-cotton blends.

Dr. Kate Goldsworthy, of the Centre for Circular Design at the University of the Arts London, introduced Rhoades to Dr. Adam Walker, a Cambridge PhD who specializes in polymer chemistry.

Basically, Rhoades said, "he takes things apart."

"We want to separate polyester and cotton," Rhoades told him.

"I can do that," he responded.

The process Walker developed is relatively straightforward. Chemical solvents are used to dissolve the polyester (like what nail polish remover and paint thinner do), until it is "a hot gooey melt" called polyester tetraacrylate—or PET. Like at Evrnu, it is extruded and chopped into pellets that look like shiny rabbit food. The pellets are sold to textile mills, where they are re-melted and spun into yarn. Worn Again does the same with the cotton that is separated from polyester.

The reason Rhoades, like Flynn, has tackled circularity of fabrics, is to "minimize impact from the beginning of the process." Reusing what we have already in hand means we take less from nature every day, and throw away less every day.

"Circular is the future," Rhoades said. "It brings fashion head-on with reality."

- - -

Perhaps the biggest name in recycled raw materials is ECONYL—"EEE-co-kneel"—a regenerated nylon made of used carpets, old fishing nets, and fabric scraps. ECONYL is the circular baby of Giulio Bonazzi, chairman and chief executive of Aquafil, a nylon manufacturer founded in Arco, Italy, in 1969.

Like polyester, nylon is petroleum-based. Because Aquafil is located close to Lake Garda—Italy's largest— Bonazzi told me, "we were always careful not to create too much environmental damage and we wanted to be eco-efficient."

The company began recycling nylon waste in the 1990s; in 2007, it started exploring how to recycle *all* nylon. "Of course, being less bad is always better," Bonazzi said. "But we wanted to change to being good."

After four years of research and development, Aquafil unveiled ECONYL.

Like Evrnu and Worn Again, Bonazzi said, "We take waste from all over the place." For fishing nets—there are some 640,000 tons of abandoned nets in our oceans— Aquafil receives calls from as far away as Australia and New Zealand. He and his team go to fetch the nets and bring them back to the ECONYL factory. There is also, surprisingly, an enormous supply of used nylon carpeting— Aquafil collected 75 million pounds (34 million kilos) a year. And once his two new carpet collection and recycling plants open in the United States, that figure will jump to 100 million pounds (45 million kilos) annually.

Surfing star Kelly Slater was one of the first in fashion to embrace ECONYL, for his sustainable fashion brand, Outerknown. Today, you'll find ECONYL in coat linings, dance wear, and carpets. Speedo swimsuits. Adidas socks. Stella McCartney's parkas and puffers are made of ECONYL nylon. In late 2018, McCartney became an ECONYL supplier too; her Italian factories collect nylon offcuts—the bits that fall on the factory floor—and send them to the ECONYL factory to be reused.

Since the nylon regeneration process "can be done an infinite number of times," Bonazzi said, ECONYL is about as circular as you can get. "You give me this carpet, I give you the yarn to make your swimwear," he said. "You give me back your swimwear, and I give you the yarn to make your jacket."

The most basic form of circularity—one you, as a clothing wearer, can adopt easily—is repair. When you tear a piece of clothing, have it mended, or fix it yourself. By doing this, you are giving a garment a longer life.

The outdoor athletic wear brand Patagonia offers a repair service called Worn Wear. Give your wounded

Patagonia item to the company, and they'll fix it for you. "The single best thing we can do for the planet is to keep our stuff in use longer," Patagonia chief executive Rose Marcario said. "Repair reduces the need to buy more," as well as cuts "waste output and water usage."

Since 2015, Worn Wear has been on the move: Menders drive around North America in a 1991 Dodge biodiesel pickup truck with a camper top made of redwood from old wine barrels. The menders in the truck will fix anything— from Patagonia or elsewhere—you bring to them. No charge. A similar Patagonia wagon drives around Great Britain and Western Europe, and there is another in Japan.

Some fashion leaders insist that the best way to prolong the life of clothes is to wash them less, and more smartly. Levi's chief Chip Bergh says you should never wash your jeans. "After we're finished wearing something, we just automatically toss it into the laundry," he said. But "a good pair of denim doesn't really need to be washed . . . except for very infrequently." Washing machines beat up denim, wearing it out quicker. Bergh suggested you do what he does: When food drips on your pant leg, spot clean the fabric with a toothbrush.

If you find the idea of wearing unwashed jeans gross, Bert Wouters, the vice president for fabric care at the global corporation Procter & Gamble, says you can absolutely put them in the washer. But like with all of your clothes, you can follow a simple three-step process that is more sustainable, meaning less damaging to the environment:

- use a high-quality detergent
- run a short cycle with cold water
- finish with fabric conditioner

You will save energy and water, you will use less detergent, which means you'll pollute less, and, because you are spinning your clothes less in the washing machine—basically beating them up less—they will last longer. "The more you put a garment to spin in a machine, the more friction there is, the more interaction there is with harsh products," the shorter life the clothes have, Wouters explained.

And if we lengthen the life of our garments, we can save millions of gallons of water and keep millions of tons of clothing from landfill.

"It's actually pretty obvious when you think about it," he said.

Iris van Herpen's Anthozoa suit, Spring-Summer Haute Couture 2013 fashion show in Paris.
© 2013 by Don Ashby/FirstVIEW.

NINE

RAGE AGAINST THE MACHINE

For years now, we've heard about how technology is going to completely change our relationship with clothing.

Early on, the news was about "wearables"—tech you can wear, like an Apple Watch or a Fitbit.

But in recent years, fashion and science have worked together in cooler ways—in materials, like I saw at Modern Meadow and Bolt Threads; in raw material recycling, like I saw with Evrnu and Worn Again; in manufacturing and distribution, with robots and automation; and in fashion design, with 3D printing.

What is 3D?

A one-dimensional object is a line. It has only one dimension: length.

A two-dimensional object is flat, like this page you are reading right now. It has two dimensions: length and width.

A three-dimensional object is solid, like a cube, a ball, a cone, or this book. A 3D object has three dimensions: length, width, and depth.

Therefore, 2D printing is what you normally think of

as printing: flat, on a piece of paper. Three-dimensional printing produces a solid object.

Though it sounds like something out of a science-fiction story about the future, it's not. Three-dimensional printing, or "additive manufacturing," has been around for a long time.

It was invented in the 1980s—the first version by a Japanese lawyer at the Nagoya Municipal Industrial Research Institute; the second, by engineers in France; and finally, by an American engineer named Chuck Hall, who printed a nifty eye-washing cup. Since then, automobile, medical, and architecture industries have all used 3D printing. In automobile production: engine parts, dashboards, front grills. In medicine: bone replacement parts, like a new knee or hip; surgical instruments; dental work such as crowns; prosthetics, such as fake hands or legs for amputees; and casts for broken bones. In architecture: building models.

Today, three-dimensional printing has the potential to change everything—and it could happen sooner than you think. Ray Kurzweil, a famous futurist who correctly predicts new trends, believes, "It will become the norm for people to have [3D] printers in their homes."

In this 3D printer future, fashion brands—from Amazon to Chanel—won't sell you actual clothes; you'll buy an internet link, click on it, and be able to print the garment yourself.

Imagine how 3D printing fashion would change everything in the fashion industry. Clothes would be designed and produced completely differently, with 3D printing, rather than sewing, in mind. Manufacturing jobs would be more high tech, and therefore safer and cleaner, like those laser jobs at Jeanologia. There would be so much less waste, because clothes would be made to order—*you'd* make the item, when you wanted it, to your size. Anywhere. Anytime. There wouldn't be leftover clothes on a sales rack, or later burned or shredded or thrown away. We'd only make what we would use.

Andrew Bolton, the head curator of the Metropolitan Museum of Art's Costume Institute, believes 3D printing could bring changes to the fashion industry "as radical as the sewing machine" did nearly two hundred years ago.

For a long time, fashion, with its emphasis on hand craftsmanship on the high end and cheap labor on the low end, paid no attention to 3D printing.

That all changed when Dutch couturier Iris van Herpen decided to start experimenting with 3D printing, and fashion took notice.

I met Iris (pronounced "EEE-reece") two weeks after her thirty-fourth birthday, in Amsterdam, on the very cold second day of summer in 2018. We were sitting at a worn wood table in her design studio in an old warehouse on the water. In the nineteenth century, this was where chocolate, cocoa, coffee, and tea arrived by ship from Africa, Asia, and South America. Now the building is a home for makers and creators such as metalsmiths, piano tuners, and van Herpen.

Van Herpen loves using technology to design and produce fashion. There are times when her designs don't even look like clothes—at least not the sort of clothes that hang in your closet or you'd wear in the street. Like the 3D creation that was on a mannequin next to us: a short dress covered with a cloud of paper-thin metal bubbles the size of baseballs. Picture what you would look like if you were dropped into a glass of ginger ale and you get the idea.

Van Herpen began experimenting with 3D printing in 2009. The first 3D printed garment she made was a short white jacket in swirling shapes, like a nautilus seashell. The jacket was stone hard and it covered the shoulders like a turtle shell. It took seven straight days and nights to complete the printing. "I thought, If this works, I will show it; if it doesn't work, it was a nice experiment," van Herpen told me. It worked.

"With 3D, I could do any texture, any complexity, in any shape," she said. There was so much choice, in fact, "I felt like, I don't know what to do!"

But because 3D printing is so expensive, and it is printed all in one go, the process forced her to "decide the final look before it's made," she explained. She had no chance to make last-minute tweaks and adjustments, like she does with clothes made of fabric. "The piece comes out of the machine completely finished. It's like a birth."

Excited by 3D printing's possibilities, van Herpen continued to play. In 2011, she created a white 3D-printed dress that curled around the body like a wide lacy ribbon and a white "skeleton" dress that looked like a Day of the Dead costume.

In late 2012, van Herpen contacted Neri Oxman, an American Israeli architect, inventor, and designer who works at Massachusetts Institute of Technology's Media Lab. Oxman has also been experimenting with 3D printing. Van Herpen explained to Oxman that she wanted to make a "fully flexible" 3D-printed dress for her next couture show in Paris in late January and asked for help. Oxman agreed.

Van Herpen designed a bell-shaped miniskirt and mini-poncho top, both covered with short, waxy, black-and-white tentacles, like those of a sea anemone. She sent sketches and photos to Oxman in Massachusetts, and the MIT team began file-making. For two months, they worked on the project by Skype and email, right through the end-of-year holidays. Tests were printed at MIT, and the ensemble was finally produced by a 3D printing company in Minnesota. It was the first time that color was included in the print, rather than as an after-treatment, like dyeing.

The outfit was called "Anthozoa 3D Skirt and Cape," and it is considered fashion's first 3D-printed high-fashion dress.

"That dress was surely a big step forward," van Herpen told me.

While van Herpen and Oxman were creating "Anthozoa" in Holland and Massachusetts, the Los Angeles–based jewelry, decor, and stage wear designer Michael Schmidt was designing and producing the first 3D-printed dress that would be flexible and move with the body, like fabric does.

Schmidt had known about 3D printing since the 1980s. He would attend NASA technology conferences in Los Angeles, and the researchers would present and explain the scientific innovations they developed for space. One of the processes was 3D printing. "You could really see this was the future," Schmidt said.

We were sitting on old metal barstools in his studio—a treasure-cave-like space in a 1930s warehouse in LA's Arts District. The workbenches around us were cluttered with cups full of pliers and blowtorches. Tools were hanging on the walls. A pair of silver plastic skeletons slouched on the sofa. Schmidt's assistants were putting finishing touches on Halloween costumes for the game show *The Price Is Right.*

A Kansas City native, Schmidt is one of the most in-demand fashion and decor designers in Los Angeles. Over the years, he has created concert tour looks for Cher, Madonna, Beyoncé, Rihanna, Janet Jackson, and Lady Gaga.

In late 2012, one of Schmidt's clients, the Ace Hotel in New York, called and asked if he would like to 3D print a garment for a technology conference they were hosting during New York Fashion Week in March.

"Yes," he said. "Now is the time to do it."

"Iris had already been doing things with 3D printing" in Amsterdam, he told me, "and I was in love with her work. But it was more sculptural. I wanted to introduce motility, I wanted to print a fabric, which had not been done, and I wanted to create an epic moment. To do that, I immediately thought of my friend Dita Von Teese," a fashion icon who works regularly with fashion designers.

Schmidt asked Von Teese, and he said, "She was super into it. So I went back to the Ace Hotel team and said, 'I'm going to do something here that no one has ever seen before.'"

Schmidt drew a Maleficent-like black gown, made of oversized mesh, like a fishnet. He emailed the sketch and Von Teese's measurements to Francis Bitonti, a New

York–based architect and expert in computer-aided design, or CAD. Like van Herpen and Oxman, they collaborated via Skype. "Francis built a virtual Dita in his computer," Schmidt said, "and we draped the material on her in real time." Schmidt sees CAD programmers as "the new tailors" of fashion.

The dress was made of nylon powder and printed in sections. "We started receiving these boxes of these weird shapes and flexible mesh and we had to link them together by hand," he said. "It was the most unnerving way of working I've ever done. Terrifying really, because we had one shot to get it right."

In all, the gown has three thousand moving joints. Everything was white; when Schmidt finished putting it together, he dyed the dress black and decorated it with more than fifty thousand Swarovski crystals. "It needed some shimmer," he explained.

To wear the dress, Von Teese steps into it, and it is laced up the back. "The first time we had her over to try it on, I wasn't a hundred percent certain that we had nailed it," Schmidt admitted. "But sure enough, it really did work. She could move in it, and walk in it, and dance in it."

"It feels like nothing else I've ever worn—that's for sure," Von Teese told me, with a laugh.

Von Teese introduced the gown at the Ace Hotel conference. Afterward, Schmidt and the dress went on a world tour, with stops at museums and tech expositions, where he retold its story.

What he finds amazing is how fast 3D technology has advanced since 2008. Now "we 3D prototype our jewelry and some sculptural work," he said. "The beauty of it is that you can create forms that are unimaginable, uncreatable in any other way."

With their high-tech experiments, van Herpen and Schmidt have pushed creativity and innovation in fashion forward. They have broken rules. They have turned crazy dreams into reality. And each time they do this, technology evolves and becomes more accessible. Today, fashion designers use 3D printing to make hats, underwear, parts of running shoes, eyeglasses, handbag closures, shoe buckles. Now we can all put on a pair of 3D-printed shades.

These brave, bold designers encourage others to challenge the system and to modernize clothing design, production, and usage in a way no one dared to consider before.

And they do so for a just reason: the betterment of all.

Many believe that tech—robots, basically—will eventually put an end to the horrible jobs of Cottonopolis, Triangle Shirtwaist, Tazreen, and Rana Plaza. Factories can be more like the tidy, quiet, air-conditioned Jeanologia workshop I saw in Ho Chi Minh City.

But is all tech good?

While working on this book, I heard every argument for and against robot technology in clothing production.

Robots will eliminate jobs that poor garment workers need, and destroy the economies of developing nations, like Bangladesh, where they live and work.

Robots will create better jobs, improve worker skills, and lift those economies to higher levels.

Robots will eliminate waste.

Robots will produce more clothes than we could ever think of wearing.

In every conversation, there were two points everyone agreed on:

Robots are coming.

And they will radically change how our clothes are made and sold.

Like 3D printing, the notion of robots is not new.

The American automobile industry has been using robots to build cars since the 1970s. Robots have been performing surgery in hospitals for more than twenty years. But it took the US Department of Defense to bring robots to fashion.

Around 2010, a team of former researchers from Georgia Tech's Advanced Technology Development Center began to experiment with robots for sewing. This was the same group of scientists who helped develop self-driving cars. They believed that the technology that keeps cars in their lane on the road could also guide robots to sew a straight line. They had been sad to see Georgia's apparel manufacturing industry collapse after NAFTA went into effect and all the factory jobs moved to Mexico and other offshore destinations with cheap labor. The scientists wondered if robotized factories might bring garment manufacturing back to Georgia.

Rightshoring, in a word.

In 2012, the scientists got a $1.26 million grant from the Department of Defense's Defense Advanced Research Projects Agency (DARPA)—the unit that helped launch the internet and self-driving automobiles—to invent sewing robots. The Department of Defense liked the project because there are roughly 1.3 million active-duty military members, and they all need uniforms. American law states that all US military uniforms must be produced in the United States. American garment workers are paid by the hour; robots are not. The uniforms, therefore, would cost less to produce. Even the government looks for ways to cut costs.

Palaniswamy "Raj" Rajan, an India-born, American-educated businessman based in Atlanta, Georgia, heard about the project. With his company SoftWear Automation, and a few other partners, he took the sewing robots that the Georgia Tech scientists had invented, and "turned it from a science project into a commercial product," he told me. He named the sewing robots "Sewbots."

Sewbots do not look human. They are box-shaped machines attached to overhead tracks, and they dart up and down the production table, sewing. To program the bots' movements, the researchers studied "how a seamstress actually operates," Rajan explained. "The first thing [sewers] do is use their eyes," and based on what they see, they manipulate the fabric. The Sewbots have computer vision that sees the cloth, decides where to sew, then copies those human movements to sew a seam.

Two years later, in 2014, SoftWear installed Sewbots in a north Georgia factory and began producing bath mats and towels. "Walmart, Bed, Bath and Beyond—you buy a Made in the USA bath mat, and it'll probably be ours," Rajan said.

In 2017, SoftWear signed a deal with Tianyuan Garments Company, a Chinese clothing manufacturer that is a major supplier for the athletic wear brand Adidas. Now, in a brand-new $20 million plant in Little Rock, Arkansas, Sewbots sew T-shirts and parts of blue jeans. "This is not a patriotic thing," Rajan said. "It's a business decision. The Chinese chairman told me it is cheaper for him to make T-shirts in the US with robots than in China with people." As always, the manufacturing company was looking for the cheapest way to produce its clothes.

"The apparel manufacturing model as it has existed for two hundred years is fundamentally broken," Rajan explained. "You are producing goods that you don't even know if people are going to buy," and doing so on the other side of the planet.

"How do you become more efficient?" he asked. And how do you reduce waste?

By producing locally, and on-demand, which means making clothes when they are ordered.

Sewbots can be programmed to change sewing patterns from outfit to outfit, and they are more accurate than humans—committing mistakes only 0.7 percent of the time. This all makes for less waste.

Rajan believes Sewbots will bring production back to the United States, the United Kingdom, France, Japan—countries that lost all their manufacturing jobs to off-shoring. Which is just what the Georgia Tech scientists wanted to do when they started the sewing robot project in 2010.

And Rajan thinks that Sewbots will eliminate the terrible, dangerous, poorly paid jobs that nobody wants, or should have to do. "The age of cheap labor is going to end," he said.

Sewbots won't put an end to *all* garment production

jobs. There will be workers tending to the robots, inspecting finished clothes, overseeing packaging and shipping. Like in the denim factory I visited in Vietnam, where the workers were running the Jeanologia laser machines, these jobs will be cleaner and safer than those in old-style sewing factories. *Much* better jobs.

And there will always be the need for accomplished sewers to do specialty work, like embroidery, and hand-stitching, and precise fittings. We won't lose those valuable skills, or beautiful craftsmanship. There will always be couture.

Sewbots, Rajan assured me, "will never do a bridal dress."

Playing mini-golf on Selfridges's roof garden.

© 1930 by General Photographic Agency/Getty Images.

TO BUY OR NOT TO BUY

Americans now spend more time on digital media than working or sleeping. Much of that time they are looking at or buying fashion. In 2017, apparel was the number two category in US e-retail sales, after consumer electronics, such as phones and computers.

Even so, people still love the act of shopping. According to a study by the National Retail Federation in 2017, 67 percent—or two-thirds—of consumers under the age of twenty-one prefer hitting what they call "physical stores" rather than shopping on the web.

The Center for Media Research reported in 2013 that shopping had become "America's favorite pastime."

"The expectation is to keep up with the ever-changing trends—[to] respond to the constant noise that says 'Come buy something else,'" Dilys Williams, director of the Centre for Sustainable Fashion at the London College of Fashion, told me.

She calls that excitable feeling when we get to the cash register to buy a new item of clothing: "the thrill of the till."

We shop a lot. Shoppers today buy five times more clothing now than they did in 1980. In 2018, that averaged sixty-eight garments a year. As a whole, the world's citizens acquire 80 billion clothing items annually.

But how did shopping for fashion become such an addiction?

Why do we buy so many clothes?

Modern retailing, like modern fashion, was born in Paris in the mid-nineteenth century, when French entrepreneur Aristide Boucicaut took an existing shop called Le Bon Marché (pronounced "luh bon mar-SHAY") and reinvented it as a big, modern department store. Le Bon Marché was the first to advertise in newspapers. The first to put price tags on items; before, the shopkeeper told you the price. It was the first to accept exchanges and returns. Customers in the store were not pressured by sales assistants to buy. You could browse freely, for fun.

In 1869, Boucicaut constructed a bigger, better version of Le Bon Marché. Taking up an entire city block, it stood four stories and was topped with a glass atrium. (It is still there, about one block from my home, where I am writing this right now. It is a very grand store.)

Le Bon Marché kicked off the golden era of department stores. Soon there were immense and beautiful department stores in most major cities: John Wanamaker in

Philadelphia; Macy's in New York; Marshall Field and Company in Chicago; and Selfridges in London.

Selfridges was founded by Harry Gordon Selfridge, an American-born retailer who had worked at Marshall Field for twenty-five years. During a vacation in London, Selfridge noticed that the city lacked a dynamic department store such as Marshall Field in Chicago.

He moved to London, and had a six-story building constructed on Oxford Street, the city's main shopping street. The store opened in 1909. And it didn't just sell stuff. Selfridges was a circus big top in the center of the city. The store displayed the first monoplane to cross the English Channel, in 1909, and twelve thousand people came to see it. In 1925, the Scottish inventor John Logie Baird introduced on the store's floor the new technology that would eventually become television. On the roof there was a miniature golf and a women's gun club. The store was such a success, and Mr. Selfridge was known as "the chairman of shopping."

For most of the twentieth century, department stores were the preferred place to shop—in big cities, and later, in suburban malls. You could always find what you needed, and a lot of things you didn't need but you loved, right there on the shop floor.

In the 1980s and 1990s, there was a series of business

deals that led to the end of many department stores. Big chains took over smaller ones. A lot of the great, elegant downtown stores changed names—Marshall Field in Chicago and John Wanamaker in Philadelphia became Macy's. Many more closed forever.

And then came the internet, and shoppers stopped going to suburban malls. Why sit in traffic, and trudge through a mall, when you could simply click on the item you wanted on a website and have it delivered to your home? With the number of customers dwindling, suburban malls started going out of business. In 2017 alone, an estimated 8,640 mall stores closed. Many more have closed since then, the pace quickened by the COVID-19 pandemic lockdowns.

The grand city department stores that did survive have changed the way they do business. In fact, they've gone back to the Harry Gordon Selfridge way of doing business, with splashy, crowd-pleasing events. Le Bon Marché each year spotlights a different place in the world, like Japan, Brazil, Brooklyn, Los Angeles. For six to eight weeks, the store sells select items from the theme place, and has cool special events to pull customers into the store. For the Brooklyn edition, there was an old-fashioned New York–style barbershop, a tattoo shop, and "Brooklyn Amusement Park," a Cinerama-like film installation by the deejays Polo & Pan of a Coney Island–like roller coaster looping its way through the borough's urban landscape. For LA, in 2018, skateboarders tricked on a half-pipe suspended from the store's ceiling.

And, under the guidance of Selfridges Group's chairman Alannah Weston, Selfridges in London has become the most sustainable department store on Earth.

Weston is a sincere environmentalist, long involved with projects to protect the planet and animals. When she took over the running of Selfridges from her father, she brought those projects with her. "When I first presented [the idea of being more pro-environment] to the team, they were, like, why would you do that?" Weston said. "But my dad just went straight for it. He loves anything that creates a buzz."

To make it all run smoothly, Weston hired a young woman named Daniella Vega as sustainability chief. Vega constantly works to make Selfridges as green as possible. She encourages designers to try new retail concepts on the store's floor, like the ECONYL wall Stella McCartney constructed to display her handbags. When Vega realized that Selfridges sold forty thousand single-serve plastic bottles of water every year in its restaurants and food halls, she banned them and had traditional water fountains installed for customers to use. "We have to make reductions in energy, waste, and water every year," she said. As she was telling me this, a waiter set my glass of orange juice on the table. It had a plastic straw in it. "That's got to go," she said, pointing to the straw. Three months later, all plastic straws were gone from the store.

Lights are fitted with energy-saving LED bulbs. The signature yellow shopping bags are partly made of recycled disposable coffee cups. On many of the clothes and accessories dangles a grass-green tag that reads *Buying Better/Inspiring Change*. The tag explains if a product is certified organic, or uses less water, or is British made. The store plans to add notices if the items are made of "responsible leather" or are "forest friendly." There is a social media hashtag: #buyingbetter.

To spread Selfridges's environmental message, Vega and her team will share its technology and practices with competitors and brands. Their point of view is that eco-ethics is not a marketing gimmick or something that you tack onto the existing model, like adding electric windows and leather upholstery options to your new car. Instead, Vega said, it is a complete rethinking and remaking of the retail business.

"Boxing sustainability in a corner and not having it throughout the store—that, for me, is not sustainable," she says. "I dream of the day I can walk through the store and the message is in every brand I pass."

Hopefully, other department stores will follow

Selfridges's lead, and all shopping can become just as sustainable.

But what if you don't have so much money to spend on clothes? What if you want to dress in the things you see at Selfridges, but you are more on an H&M budget? What do you do?

I thought back to what designer Stella McCartney said when I initially asked her about this: "If you can't afford it the first time around, get it in the sale. Get it in the sale of the sale of the sale. Get it secondhand."

Secondhand means buying something that once belonged to someone else, like a used car. You can also buy used clothing. They are normally sold two ways: at a secondhand store, which is usually filled with clothes people have donated; or on consignment, which is filled with clothes people are selling themselves, with the help of the shop owner. With consignment, the person selling the clothes gets a portion of the price paid, and the shop owner gets the rest.

For a long time, secondhand shops were filled with dowdy clothes. Most customers were either down on their luck, or students who had no money. (I loved the Salvation Army's dollar skirt rack when I was a college student.)

But around the year 2000, secondhand clothing got a new

name: "vintage," like an old wine. And like an old wine, it was thought that the older these clothes got, the better they were. Hollywood actresses started wearing vintage dresses and suits for their red-carpet looks. For the 2001 Academy Awards, the movie star Renée Zellweger wore a beautiful canary-yellow chiffon gown by French couturier Jean Dessès, made in 1959, and Julia Roberts wore a glamorous black-and-white gown by Valentino from 1992. Old became new again. Secondhand was now chic. "Hollywood and fashionable people realized the greenness of vintage," Cameron Silver, founder and owner of the West Hollywood vintage boutique Decades, told me. Because wearing secondhand was so sustainable, "it became double-plus cool," he said.

Today, secondhand fashion is big business. And one of the leaders of that business is Julie Wainwright of The RealReal, an online consignment company based in San Francisco. Founded in 2011, The RealReal is a fashion lover's dream consignment shop: You can find Louis Vuitton satchels, Gucci dresses, Chanel suits, fine jewelry, all at affordable prices.

Wainwright had no fashion experience before The RealReal; she was a techie who founded Pets.com, a pet supply company that closed in 2000.

Wainwright saw millennial customers' enthusiasm for

for high fashion and eco-ethics. Given that consignment is, at its core, circular, The RealReal is both.

Wainwright's team receives items from consignees (the people who give her the clothes to sell), evaluates them from "good" to "pristine," then offers them for sale on the website. "Fifty percent of our buyers had never bought consignment until they shopped with us," she said.

At any given point, The RealReal has hundreds of thousands of items for sale, and 98 percent of that stock is sold within three months of its posting. "We've got consumers who buy from us, then they resell the next season, and then they buy again," she said. "We're getting people to circle in our own circular economy."

The first year, Wainwright did $10 million in sales. In 2019, sales topped $1 billion. According to a study of the US market, growth in resold items is expected to increase significantly—much faster than new items.

Stella McCartney, as you can imagine, is 100 percent behind it. "Resale is a way of generating business without needing to continually create new materials and extract resources from the planet," she told me.

And what if you were to skip the notion of ownership entirely? What if you stopped buying clothes and rented them instead?

Renting clothes for men is not a radical idea. My high school boyfriend rented his tux for the prom. My husband rented his formal three-piece morning suit and top hat for our wedding.

But women? For anything other than a costume party? Unthinkable.

Why?

Because the fashion industry has always wanted women to buy. How else could it keep the cycle going and the profits rolling in?

Then, along came the sharing economy—the idea that we don't have to possess something to use it. We share cars (Uber and Lyft), music (Spotify), homes (AirBnB). It was only a matter of time before we shared our clothes.

Renting clothes lets average, middle-market shoppers have access (at least briefly) to the same level of luxury and style that the wealthy always have, and they can get it right now, for a fraction of the high retail price. The only items you'd ever need to buy are underwear, sleepwear, swimwear, and shoes. Renting, more than any other business model in the apparel industry, gives as many people as possible the chance to wear "fashion." And to do so daily.

Unquestionably the leader in garment sharing is the New York–based Rent the Runway. Founded in 2009 by a pair of Harvard Business School students, Jennifer

Hyman and Jennifer Fleiss, it focused for nearly ten years on special-occasion clothes such as prom gowns and party dresses—the non-celebrity version of red-carpet dressing. It wasn't easy to get brands on board. Many were worried that renting could kill their sales. When Rent the Runway approached New York–based designer Derek Lam about carrying his fashion on the website for rent, his chief executive Jan-Hendrik Schlottmann wondered if making the clothes so available would cheapen the company's reputation.

But then Schlottmann realized that "the Rent the Runway customer is not a customer we're losing," he said. "She's not going to spend fifteen hundred dollars on a dress." No, she's the customer who goes to fast-fashion stores and buys knockoffs. Putting the originals on Rent the Runway at roughly the same price could be a way to fight back. Consider Mary Katrantzou's ongoing war with counterfeiters. I googled her name and *rent,* and up popped girlmeetsdress.com, a British fashion rental site, with a few of her digital printed dresses renting for £49 (or $62).

Well done, I thought. If women can rent Katrantzou's design at the same price as its rip-off—and love it so much more—maybe the rip-off market will shrivel up and die.

Rent the Runway's ambition, Hyman said, is to "put Zara and H&M out of business."

It very well might. Renting fashion could change the entire shape of the apparel industry. If people rent clothes, instead of buying them, fewer clothes would need to be made, and what is out there could be circulated more, and thrown away less.

Workers wouldn't have to put in overtime, unpaid. There would be no need for sweatshops. There would be less over-farming, less over-production, less pollution, less waste. Less thievery from designers like Mary Katrantzou. Less tragedy, like Rana Plaza. Less clothing thrown into landfill. Fashion would be less destructive to the planet and to humanity.

Wanting to give the rental approach a try myself, I went to see Panoply (pronounced "PAN-o-plee"), a luxury-fashion rental company in Paris founded by two French entrepreneurs, Ingrid Brochard and Emmanuelle Brizay. I learned about Panoply from Stella McCartney. She had her clothes available to rent there.

Brochard and Brizay met through mutual friends and decided to go into business together. They began to ponder the sharing economy, and how it could affect fashion. They decided renting clothes was the answer.

They started Panoply in early 2016. From the beginning, they carried well-known labels, and rental price included delivery, pickup, and dry cleaning with an ecocleaner—one that avoids using harmful chemicals. Delivery in Paris was by bicycle messenger.

I went to see them in the fall of 2018. The following week, I was attending a conference in London, at the Centre for Sustainable Fashion, and thought it would be cool to rent my outfit. Panoply stylist Bettina Hetoubanabo, a thirty-year-old Parisienne, took me in hand. "Selling is so old-fashioned," she told me as she handed me a Stella McCartney navy wool suit with an oversized hot-pink plaid. "Renting is the new way to see things."

With the boxy jacket and the cropped trousers, in such a lively plaid, the suit was not something I would have ever chosen on my own. And at the retail price of €1,720 (roughly $2,000), it was far beyond what I could afford. But to rent it at €255 (or $300)? That was doable.

It was delivered by bike the next day, and off to London it went with me. During the conference, I got a lot of compliments. When I responded that I'd rented it, I got *more* compliments. How sustainable! How circular!

The day after the sustainability conference, I returned to Paris.

And the day after that, around noon, the Panoply courier came to my flat and picked up the garment bag.

The suit was gone.

I was sad.

I liked it. A lot.

I could imagine buying it, including it in my wardrobe, in my life.

Then I decided: No, it was right for it to go back.

I could live without it.

After all, there would always be another.

EPILOGUE

Most of the people I met on my journey writing this book have different approaches to sustainability and ethical behavior in fashion. There was slow fashion, and rightshoring, and green fashion, and the high tech of 3D printing and robots. But one thing was clear: Today, the fashion industry is a complex and epic-sized mess, and it's going to take *all* of their approaches, and many others, to tackle it and build a better, fairer fashion ecosystem.

Everyone spotlighted in this book is, in their way, fighting a model that is completely unsustainable. One that celebrates endless consumption, ever lower prices (whether achieved by stealing someone's art or their human rights), and ever larger profits. That purposely produces leftovers. That gives no thought at all to the destruction it causes on the environment.

But the revolution is not only going to come from the makers. We all have to step up. Buy less. Wash our clothes differently. Repair them more. Think about the impact of the material they are made of. Think about the supply chain that produces them. Think about the beliefs of the company that created and sold them. We need to support fashion that does more good for the world than ill.

HERE IS WHAT YOU CAN DO:

LAUNDER YOUR CLOTHES LESS FREQUENTLY

Try to break the habit of tossing a pair of jeans into the laundry after wearing them once. Get several wears out of clothes before washing, spot-clean small stains, and use cold, short washing cycles. You'll reduce water usage, cut your parents' household expenses, and elongate your clothes' lifespans.

SHOP YOUR CLOSET

Before asking your parents to buy a new pair of jeans or another black T-shirt, look inside your closet to see if you already have those pieces. Or try gathering some friends for a clothing swap party.

RENT YOUR WARDROBE

There's a growing number of websites and programs today that make it easy for people of all ages to rent beautiful clothes for everything from regular days to special occasions, like weddings. Get your parents to rent their party clothes. Some sites even specialize in kids' clothes! Renting reduces waste.

TAKE A SECOND LOOK AT SECONDHAND

For a long time, consignment shops were filled with old, dowdy clothes—but no more. Today, you'll find great deals on cool clothes in thrift shops and on consignment websites.

CONSIGN ONLINE

Have any gently worn garments hanging in your closet that you've outgrown? Tell your parents to consign them online. They'll make some money back, and your clothes will have a second life.

SKIP THE PLASTIC BAGS

You may be in the habit of taking your canvas tote to the grocery store or farmer's market. Don't forget to take it along when shopping for clothes as well.

REPAIR AND RE-WEAR

Rather than tossing out stained or torn garments, think about overdyeing, or covering the stain or hole with cool embroideries. Such treatments personalize items—making them one of a kind!—and give them a longer life.

PICK UP A NEEDLE YOURSELF

Learn to sew or knit, and make or repair your own clothes. You can easily find classes on YouTube.

LEAD WITH YOUR BEST FOOT FORWARD

Instead of throwing away your gently used shoes, seek out a local charity organization that can give the shoes to communities that may need them.

GLOSSARY

ADVOCATE: a person who works on other people's behalf

ANTI-CORRUPTION COMMISSION: a group of people working to prevent or stop dishonest behavior

APPAREL: clothing

BANKRUPTCY: a situation where a person or company officially cannot pay their debts, which is money they owe. In business, the company will often be forced to close, or be sold, to pay off the debts.

BESPOKE: clothes that are made for a particular customer, usually men, and often sewed by hand

BIODIESEL: diesel fuel made of plants or animals

BIOFABRICATION: the production of natural materials in a laboratory

BIOREACTOR: a tank or container in a laboratory used for chemical experiments

BIOTECHNOLOGY: the science of using living organisms to create things, like using yeast to make bread

BOLL: a roundish pod on a plant. For cotton, it is the fluffy white ball.

CARCINOGEN: a substance that can cause cancer

CONSIGNEE: a person selling something on consignment

COTTON GIN: a machine to separate raw cotton from its seeds

COUTURE: the design and production of fashionable clothes to a client's specific requirements and measurements. Usually for women.

CULPABLE HOMICIDE: an act in which a person is killed, but the death is not considered murder

ECO-ETHICS: the moral relationship between humans and the environment

ECONOMIC: the adjective of economy, and also related to production, distribution, and consumption of goods and services

ECONOMY: the wealth of a country or place, based on the production, distribution, and consumption of goods and services

ECOSYSTEM: a complex network, or interconnected system

EMBEDDED: a substance deeply affixed to a material

ETHICIST: a person who studies and considers moral principles that govern human behavior

EXECUTIVES: company bosses who manage or direct the business, like the president or vice president

FILTRATION SYSTEM: a mechanical system that cleans air of particles

GLOBALIZATION: the phenomenon of companies and organizations expanding around the world

HERBICIDE: a chemical substance that kills weeds

HYPERLOCAL: focusing on a small community or region

INSULATION: material that prevents loss of heat

MINIMUM WAGE: the lowest amount the government says you are allowed to be paid

NEGOTIATE: to reach an agreement through discussion and compromise

NOURISH: provide what's needed to be healthy and to grow

PATENT: a government-issued license that gives the applicant the sole right for a set time to make, use, or sell an invention

PETROLEUM: a liquid extracted from the Earth's core and used to make gasoline and diesel oil

POLYESTER: a silky synthetic fabric made of petroleum-based materials

POLYMERS: synthetic substances used as plastic

POLYVINYL CHLORIDE (PVC): a type of plastic, such as vinyl

POSTCONSUMER: after a consumer has used the item

PROTECTIONISM: the practice of protecting a country's businesses from foreign competition by taxing imports (this type of tax is called a "tariff")

PROTOTYPE: a sample or model of a product, built or made as a test

READY-TO-WEAR: clothes that are made for the general market and sold through stores or online, rather than made to order for an individual customer. The opposite of bespoke and couture.

SEAMSTRESSES: workers who sew clothes

SHAREHOLDER: a person who owns a portion—or share—of a company

SOLVENT: a solution that dissolves a solid, like nail polish or paint thinner

SUEDE: a velvet-textured leather

SUSTAINABILITY: avoiding the depletion of natural resources in order to maintain an ecological balance

SWEATSHOP: a factory or workshop where workers earn very low wages for long hours and under poor conditions. The term dates back to the nineteenth century, when tailors worked in such terrible conditions, they sweated on the job.

SYNTHETIC: a fabric made by a chemical process, usually to imitate a natural fabric

TANNIN: yellow or brown bitter-tasting substance in bark, roots, and other plant tissue such as grape skin and seeds

TEXTILE: cloth

VISA: a document, often in a passport, that grants permission for the holder to enter, leave, or stay for a certain amount of time in a country

VISCOSE: a soft, silk-like synthetic fabric

WELFARE: government money given to people in need

ACKNOWLEDGMENTS

This is a book about women, by women. It wouldn't exist without my Penguin editors Virginia Smith Younce and Dana Chidiac, and my agents, Tina Bennett, at Bennett Literary, and Janine Kamouh, at William Morris Endeavor, who believed in it, and me, and made it sing. My research assistants, Chantel Tattoli and Emily Wall. My fact checkers Barbara Kean, Gillian Aldrich, Leslie Wiggins, and Regina Bresler. And my junior editor, Nina Apodaca-Griffith, who read the manuscript with a keen eye, and provided sharp insight from the young reader point of view.

And most importantly, I must thank my husband and daughter, Hervé and Lucie d'Halluin, who lived through the book-writing circus yet again. They are the most courageous of all.